A HISTORY OF
PSYCHOLOGICAL TESTING

❖ ❖ ❖

Hundreds of Individual Civil Service Examination Rooms at Nanking, China. © 1927, National Geographic Society. (Photograph by Maynard Owen Williams about twenty years after testing stopped in 1905.)

A HISTORY OF
PSYCHOLOGICAL TESTING

Philip H. Du Bois

WASHINGTON UNIVERSITY
ST. LOUIS

ALLYN AND BACON, INC.
BOSTON

❖ ❖ ❖

Library of Congress Catalog Card Number: 79–113263.

Printed in the United States of America.

To those wise men of China

who, thousands of years ago,

invented the psychological test.

174598

CONTENTS

FOREWORD

The need for a short history of psychological testing became apparent a few years ago when I discovered numerous omissions and errors in published accounts, both in histories of psychology and in texts on psychometrics.

Psychometrics now has considerable autonomy both as a branch of knowledge and as a profession; therefore, it seems appropriate to attempt to trace major lines of influence in its development. I hope that this volume will interest both professional psychometricians and students in training.

The literature of psychometrics is now so vast and the number of contributors so great that topics and names must be selected. Obviously, another author attempting a historical report on the development of the field would produce a different book. As a result of spending many hours on this endeavor, my interest in the historical development of psychometrics has increased, and I know I would enjoy reading an account developed by another author. However, as far as I know, this is the first attempt to treat the history of psychometrics comprehensively.

The emphasis in all cases has been to identify innovators and those who for one reason or another have clearly influenced later developments, and therefore the work of many highly competent individuals both in earlier times and in the modern period has not been mentioned. There is also the matter of an arbitrary time limit. No researcher was considered for a portrait unless he or she made an important contribution in the field prior to the end of World War II. A future historian of psychometrics undoubtedly would wish to include many additional portraits.

Several drawings would have been included had suitable photographs been available; notably Whipple, Healy, Wells, and Knox, the inventive doctor at Ellis Island who served in the United States Army during the Mexican Campaign and later went into private practice in New Jersey.

I am indebted to Mr. Charles Biggs of St. Louis for his skill in making line drawings from photographs of forty-four of the founders of psychometrics. Dr. John A. Popplestone of the Archives of the History of American Psychology kindly supplied pictures of Witmer and Pintner, as well as a photograph from the Goddard collection of the group of psychologists who were responsible for the Army Alpha.

I am also indebted to several individuals who were kind enough to send me photographs at my request, and to Mr. Lawrence J. M. Rice of Washington, D. C., who lent me an excellent photograph of his father, the late Joseph M. Rice, the founder of modern educational testing.

Permission to reprint a picture of Galton's Laboratory was kindly given by the Cambridge University Press. The National Geographic Magazine, through Mr. Andrew Poggenpohl, art editor, made an exception to their general policy and released the photograph of the testing rooms at Nanking, China, taken many years ago by my late friend, Maynard Owen Williams. I am also indebted to the Clark University Press for releasing a passage giving Woodworth's account of the creation of the first personality questionnaire. Dr. King M. Wientge of the University of Missouri, St. Louis, and Dr. Joan F. Dixon of Washington University read the manuscript and made helpful suggestions. I am also indebted to Portia W. Jones for her careful typing of the manuscript and her assistance with numerous, demanding chores.

Philip H. DuBois

A HISTORY OF
PSYCHOLOGICAL TESTING

❖ ❖ ❖

1

EARLY
PSYCHOLOGICAL TESTING

Modern psychological testing has roots in three earlier developments: civil service examinations, the assessment of academic achievement in universities and schools, and studies by European and American scientists on the measurement of individual differences in behavior. The influence of the first two was indirect, serving chiefly to establish widespread acceptance of formal examining methods. Psychological testing, as it is known today, originated in investigations of person-to-person variability in functions such as sensory discrimination, reaction time, perceptual abilities, motor skills, and problem solving.

CIVIL SERVICE TESTING

For more than 3,000 years an elaborate system of competitive examinations was used to select personnel for government positions in China, which, unlike European countries, had no hereditary ruling class. Origins of the system go back to 2200 B.C., when the Chinese emperor examined his officials every third year to determine their fitness for continuing in office. After three examinations, officials were either promoted or dismissed.

In 1115 B.C., candidates for government posts were examined for their proficiency in the "six arts": music, archery, horsemanship, writing, arithmetic, and the rites and ceremonies of public and private life.

Later, under the Han dynasty (202 B.C.–200 A.D.), written examinations were introduced in the "five studies," civil law, military affairs, agriculture, revenue, and the geography of the Empire. Local authorities were under instructions from the Emperor to seek out and recommend capable individuals of high moral standards to take the examinations and to qualify for an appointment.

Through the centuries, the examination system underwent many changes, taking final form about the year 1370 A.D. Proficiency in remembering and interpreting the Confucian classics was emphasized. A man aspiring to high public office was required to pass three competitive examinations. The first, given annually in the chief city of the district in which the candidate lived, required a day and a night in a small isolated booth, where the candidate wrote a poem and composed an essay or two on assigned themes. Work was judged by beauty of penmanship and grace of diction; the percentage passing is reported to have been 1 per cent to 7 per cent.

Every three years competitors successful in the district examinations assembled in the provincial capitals for three sessions of three days and three nights each. Compositions in prose and verse revealed extent of reading and depth of scholarship. At this level, penmanship did not count, since a bureau of examination copyists (established in 1015 A.D.) reproduced the papers in another hand before they were evaluated by two independent readers, with a third reader to receive and reconcile the sealed grades. Successful candidates (reported as 1 per cent to 10 per cent) were considered "promoted scholars" and were admitted to the examinations given the following spring in Peking, the capital of the Empire. Here perhaps 3 per cent became mandarins, eligible for public office.

CIVIL SERVICE EXAMINATION HALLS AT PEKING,
CHINA, ABOUT 1900.

During the centuries the civil service system was in use, China had no universities or public school system. Nevertheless, demonstrated knowledge led to public honor and responsibility. The system, emphasizing classical scholarship, was important in the high degree of stability attained by the Chinese empire, which was more or less isolated from outside influences. After the Chinese came in contact with the West, the need for skills other than classical scholarship became apparent. In 1905 the examination system was abolished so that formal university training in science and other areas of modern knowledge would be accepted by Chinese aspiring to office.

As European contacts with the Far East developed in the sixteenth century and later, the Chinese system of competitive written examinations as a means of entry into the public service was admired and praised. Two liberals whose writings presaged the French Revolution, Voltaire* and Quesnay, advocated its use in France. Actually, such a system was introduced as a reform measure in 1791, only to be abolished under Napoleon and then restored many years later.

In the early part of the nineteenth century, British diplomats and missionaries visiting China became well acquainted with the Chinese examinations and suggested that something similar be tried out in the United Kingdom. Here the first use of open competitive examinations occurred in 1833 in connection with selecting trainees for the Indian civil service. Before the first British civil service commission was set up in the 1850's, it was pointed out in a debate in Parliament that the only precedent exactly applying was that of the Chinese.

CIVIL SERVICE IN THE UNITED STATES

Successful British experience led to interest in the United States in competitive examinations as a tool in substituting merit for political favoritism in public appointments. Bills to establish an examining system were introduced in Congress in the 1860's by Senator Charles Sumner of Massachusetts and Representative Thomas A. Jenckes of Rhode Island. In 1868 Mr. Jenckes submitted to Congress a 220-page report entitled "Civil Service in the United States," which included extensive descriptions of the civil service examining procedures used in China, Prussia, and France. Twelve years later, British experience and procedures were described in detail in "Civil Service in Great Britain,"

* In the *Essai sur les Moeurs*, Voltaire wrote as follows: "L'esprit humain ne peut certainement imaginer un gouvernement meilleur que celui où tout se décide par de grands tribunaux, subordonnés les uns aux autres, dont les membres ne sont reçus qu'après plusieurs examens sévères."

by Dorman B. Eaton (1880), who already had served as a chairman of the first U. S. Civil Service Board* under President Grant and who

DORMAN B. EATON (1823–1899)

A lawyer who was active in civil service reform in the United States, Mr. Eaton was president of the Civil Service Board under President Grant and an influential member of the permanent Civil Service Commission established in 1883.

later became a member of the permanent commission established under the Civil Service Act of January 16, 1883. This book was important in mobilizing American public opinion in favor of using examination results as a basis for evaluating candidates for government positions.

The act of Congress establishing competitive tests as a means of entry into the government service prescribed that "such examinations shall be practical in their character, and so far as may be shall relate to those matters which will fairly test the relative capacity and fitness of the persons examined to discharge the duties of the service into which they seek to be appointed."

The work of the Civil Service Commission is described in a continuing series of annual reports, which began in 1884. Early reports stressed the practical nature of the examinations and exhibited sample questions which do not differ greatly in intent from items used in modern tests designed to measure skill or proficiency in an occupation.

---

* The first U. S. civil service procedures applied only in certain departments. An inquiry in Congress led to the publication of the tests which had been used. The examinations were abandoned when Congress failed to make appropriations to continue them. A sample instrument of this period is given in the Appendix.

However, neither the method of requiring a person being examined to select the correct answer to a problem from among two or more alternatives nor the statistical techniques appropriate for the analysis of test results had yet been developed.

A wide array of examinations, sampling to an appreciable extent the activities in dozens of occupations, from postal clerk and draftsman to maritime meteorological expert, botanist, and physician, were developed and put to use. Both the biographical information set forth by the candidate in his application form and performance on the job during the six months probationary period were recognized as additional means of determining occupational fitness.

Technical procedures used in the early years of the commission included:

1. Study of characteristics of individuals performing successfully in positions to be filled by examination.
2. Development of examination questions intended to measure these characteristics.
3. Administration of examinations under conditions intended to give each candidate an equal opportunity to succeed.
4. The use of a system of examination numbers to conceal the identity of candidates from examiners reading the tests.
5. The use of a carefully drawn point system in the scoring of tests so that the final score would not vary appreciably with the examiner assigned to read the test. In this connection the first annual report stated: "It has been practicable to attain a high degree of uniformity and certainty in these markings."
6. Ranking the candidates in order of grade as a step in determining eligibility for appointment.

The problem of relating test results to later performance was recognized in the third annual report: "It could be shown statistically that those who pass highest in the examinations are likely to make the most useful public servants." While the evidence presented was anecdotal, numerous government administrators, including members of the President's cabinet, attested to the success of the new system in finding capable employees.

In the report for the fiscal year 1889 (the first report signed by Theodore Roosevelt, who served six years as a member of the Commission) the inclusion of up to 5 per cent of the examination questions on United States geography, government, and history was defended in these words: "Moreover, these questions are a test of a man's general intelligence." In subsequent years, however, such questions were dropped. In the words of the same annual report, "The commission emphatically asserts that the examinations are of such a character as to afford good common-sense business tests of the fitness of the applicants for the special duties of their positions."

UNIVERSITY AND SCHOOL EXAMINATIONS

No formal examinations are known to have existed in the schools of Greece and Rome or in the cathedral and monastery schools of medieval Europe. Although university practices in the later middle ages varied widely, degrees came into existence as formal authorization to teach, and university examinations appeared (centuries after Chinese civil service testing was well developed) as a means of determining eligibility for a degree. For hundreds of years university examinations were exclusively oral. Perhaps the earliest formal examinations were those in law at the University of Bologna in 1219. In these examinations a real test of competence was conducted in private, followed by a public examination which was essentially a formality.

Also in the thirteenth century, formal oral examinations before the chancellor and several doctors were described by the chaplain of Louis IX, Robert de Sorbon, who in 1257 founded the community of masters and students that eventually evolved into the Sorbonne.

Louvain University had competitive examinations as early as 1441 (sixteen years after its founding), in which candidates were arranged in four classes: "rigorosi" (honor men), "transibiles" (satisfactory), "gratiosi" (charity passes), and failures. The examination system at Louvain helped to establish its outstanding academic reputation.

The development of written examinations in European schools followed the introduction of paper, which in the twelfth century began to replace papyrus and parchment as a writing medium. Paper-making, an ancient Chinese invention, was acquired by the Arabs, who in 751 A.D. found paper-makers among Chinese prisoners captured in an attack on Samarkand. Centuries later, Europeans learned the art from the Arabs in contacts in the Middle East during the Crusades and in Sicily and Spain.

Members of the Jesuit order, founded in 1540 by St. Ignatius of Loyola, were pioneers in the systematic use of written tests, both for the placement of students and for their evaluation after instruction. The "Ratio Studiorum," a document prescribing educational procedures on both secondary and higher levels, was published in definitive form in 1599, after several preliminary drafts. It contains the following rules for the conduct of examinations in the lower schools (McGucken, 1932):

1. All should know that absentees on the day assigned for composition will receive no consideration unless they are detained for weighty reasons.

2. All should be present in the classroom in good time to receive the assignment and instructions, given either by the prefect himself or his substitute, and they must finish the assignment before the end of school. After silence has been enjoined, no one may speak to another, not even to the prefect or his substitute.

3. All should come supplied with books and necessary writing materials so there may be no need to borrow anything during the writing period.

4. The writing should be done in a style befitting the grade of each class, clearly, and in the words of the assigned theme and according to the fashion prescribed. Ambiguous expressions are to be given the less favorable meaning. Words omitted or changed carelessly for the sake of avoiding a difficulty are to be counted as errors.

5. Care should be taken that no copying be done by bench mates; if two compositions are found to be exactly alike, both of them are to be suspected since it is impossible to discover which of the two did the copying.

6. To prevent dishonesty, anyone who has permission to leave the room after the writing has commenced should be obliged to leave the assignment and whatever he has written with the prefect or with the one who is presiding.

7. After the composition is finished, each one, without leaving his place, should diligently look over what he has written, correct and improve it as much as he may wish. For, as soon as the composition is given to the prefect, if anything then has to be corrected, it should by no means be returned.

8. Each one must fold his composition according to the directions of the prefect and write on the back his full name in Latin. Thus all the compositions may be more easily arranged in alphabetical order if desired.

9. When a student brings his finished composition to the prefect, he should take his books with him and depart quietly. The students that remain should not change their places but finish their work at their own desks.

10. If anyone should not finish his composition in the allotted time, he should hand in what he has written. On this account, all should clearly know how much time is granted for writing, rewriting and revision.

11. Finally, when they go to the oral examination, let them bring with them the texts explained that year which constitute the matter for examination. While one is being examined, the others present should pay strict attention; they must, however, neither prompt the one being examined nor correct him unless told to do so.

UNIVERSITY EXAMINATIONS IN ENGLAND

In England, oral examinations for both the B.A. and M.A. degrees were introduced at Oxford in 1636, under the statutes of Chancellor William Laud, later to be Archbishop of Canterbury and an important figure in the English Civil War. A new statute in 1800, dealing specifically with examinations, led to an honors program, emphasizing high levels of proficiency in areas such as literature and mathematics. Written examinations were used at Oxford at least as early as 1803 (and at Cambridge considerably earlier), while printed question papers were introduced in 1828. The University of London was chartered in 1836 to examine candidates for degrees from two London colleges, and later opened its examinations to externs as well. In actuality, for many years the University of London was purely an examining and degree-conferring organization, having no instructional program of its own.

The success of the English universities in using written examinations to improve teaching and student achievement was undoubtedly a factor in the interest of English statesmen, including Lord Macaulay and William E. Gladstone, in the use of written examinations for the selection of government personnel. By the middle of the nineteenth century, written examinations had been recognized in England, on the Continent, and in the United States as an appropriate basis for important decisions: who should be awarded degrees; who should be permitted to exercise a profession, such as law or teaching or medicine; and who should serve in a government post.

The foundations for the invention of the psychological test had been laid. Techniques for assessing the results of training were well established. Steps had been taken toward developing uniformity of testing situations and objectivity of appraisal. Still to come were the extension of measurement to other areas of human behavior, the invention of novel methods of measurement, formulation of concepts relating to the practice and theory of testing, and the discovery of statistical techniques with which to analyze and describe quantitative results. The time was ripe for developments by pioneers such as Francis Galton in England, James McKeen Cattell in the United States, Emil Kraepelin in Germany, and Alfred Binet in France.

SIR FRANCIS GALTON

Sir Francis Galton (1822–1911), who became a principal founder of the scientific study of human differences, was originally trained in medicine at Kings College, London; Trinity College, Cambridge; and

SIR FRANCIS GALTON (1822–1911)

Discoverer of correlation and regression, Galton developed the first battery of tests for the study of individual differences in psychological functions (1884). Galton also invented the questionnaire and devised a stop watch for use in investigating association.

at hospitals in Birmingham and London. Upon inheriting a comfortable fortune at the age of twenty-two, he abandoned his medical studies and spent several years traveling and leading the life of an English country gentleman. Eventually his curiosity and his vigor of intellect led him to more than half a century of wide-ranging, creative scholarship.

In two years in southwest Africa he made important contributions to geography. (As an African explorer Galton was a contemporary of David Livingstone.) Later, he was the first to publish weather maps and to describe the anticyclone as a weather system. He developed a method of composite photography for summarizing portraits, as on ancient coins. He carried out the scientific work that led to the use of fingerprints as a means of identification. Human heredity became the field in which he combined his interests in anthropology, psychology, and statistics. He pioneered in the study of resemblance in physical and mental characteristics in successive generations, and he used twins to investigate the relative effects of nurture and nature. He recognized the need for a method to describe the relationship between two variables, and it was within the framework proposed by Galton that Karl Pearson later developed the product-moment formula for linear correlation now in universal use.

While Galton foresaw that measurements of individual differences could be used in practical situations, such as selecting employees, he was interested in psychological tests primarily as tools in his scientific studies. In 1883 he summarized several years of investigations in a book entitled "Inquiries into Human Faculty and its Development." Among the novel measurement techniques described were: a set of blocks of identical appearance but of weight varying in a geometric series devised to measure ability to discriminate weights; a variable-pitch whistle for determining the upper limit of audible sound in different persons (subsequently known as the Galton Whistle); and a questionnaire on visual images that he had devised (quite probably the first use of the questionnaire in psychological research).

FRANCIS GALTON'S FIRST ANTHROPOMETRIC LAB-ORATORY AT THE INTERNATIONAL HEALTH EXHI-BITION, SOUTH KENSINGTON, 1884–5. (Photograph courtesy of Cambridge University Press.)

Galton reported two surprising discoveries. One was that blind individuals, contrary to popular belief at the time, have no greater tactual or auditory sensitivity than the sighted. The other was that scientists as a group have much poorer visual imagery than nonscientists.

In 1884, in connection with the International Health Exhibition in London, Galton opened an Anthropometric Laboratory, where for a small fee a person could have a series of measurements taken and recorded. Certain measures were of static characteristics: standing height, sitting height, arm span, and weight. Others involved behavior: vital or breathing capacity, strength of pull, strength of squeeze, swiftness of blow, keenness of sight, memory of form, discrimination of color, and steadiness of hand.

An 1884 announcement read, in part, as follows:

This laboratory is established by Mr. Francis Galton for the following purposes:

1. For the use of those who desire to be accurately measured in many ways, either to obtain timely warning of remediable faults in development, or to learn their powers.

2. For keeping a methodical register of the principal measurements of each person, of which he may at any future time obtain a copy under reasonable restrictions. His initials and date of birth will be entered in the register, but not his name. The names are indexed in a separate book.

3. For supplying information on the methods, practice, and uses of human measurement.

4. For anthropometric experiment and research, and for obtaining data for statistical discussion.

Charges for making the principal measurements: Threepence each, to those who are already on the Register. Fourpence each, to those who are not; one page of the Register will thenceforward be assigned to them, and a few extra measurements will be made, chiefly for future identification.

The Superintendent is charged with the control of the laboratory and with determining in each case, which, if any, of the extra measurements may be made, and under what conditions.

After the Health Exhibition closed, the laboratory was re-established at the Science Museum, South Kensington. All together some ·9,337 males and females, ranging in age from five to eighty, were measured on seventeen variables. Galton utilized some of the data in developing tables of percentile norms, by sex, for several physical and behavioral characteristics, including height, weight, strength, and keenness of sight. More importantly, the existence of a mass of unreduced data stimulated Galton to develop correlation as a tool in understanding imperfect relationships between variables. A decade after Galton's death investigators were still analyzing the information he had gathered. His Anthropometric Laboratory was the forerunner of similar testing at universities in England and the United States.

In the area of psychological testing, Galton was a pioneer in the development of measuring devices to investigate psychological problems, including age and sex differences in behavior. He also spent considerable effort on the development of scales, so as to reduce to meaningful and orderly numbers characteristics such as skin pigmentation and hair color. However, his most outstanding contribution to what later became the area of test theory was, without doubt, the development of the concept of correlation.

KARL PEARSON

For Karl Pearson (1857–1936), psychological measurement had only tangential appeal. Appointed at the age of twenty-seven to the professorship of applied mathematics and mechanics at University College, London, he demonstrated broad scientific interests, which eventually focused on evolution, biological inheritance, eugenics, and the development of statistical methods. He used statistical methods primarily to investigate problems of heredity, but he was so successful that he may be considered the founder of mathematical statistics. His work was supported, in part, by gifts to the college from the Worshipful Company of Drapers (one of the ancient chartered associations of the City of London) and by Francis Galton, who provided a substantial sum in 1904 for the founding of what became the Eugenics Laboratory. Galton eventually left his fortune to the college to establish the Galton professorship of eugenics. Pearson was the first incumbent; R. A. Fisher—perhaps the most creative statistician of modern times—was the second.

In addition to the product-moment formula for r, Pearson's most useful contributions to psychological measurement include multiple correlation, methods for finding correlations from fourfold tables, biserial r, correction of correlations for changes in range, and the chi

KARL PEARSON (1857–1936)

Many statistical concepts useful in psychological measurement stem from Pearson's work, including product-moment correlation, multiple R, partial r and the phi coefficient. He was a close friend and biographer of Galton, to whom he gave full credit for the original conceptualization of correlation.

square test for goodness of fit. This list includes versions of many of the statistics used routinely in test development to this day.

CATTELL'S BATTERIES OF TESTS

The American psychologist who introduced the Galton tradition in testing to the United States and who was responsible for many early developments in mental measurement was James McKeen Cattell (1860–1944). After graduating from Lafayette College in 1880, he studied philosophy abroad and at Johns Hopkins, where he also began "psychometric" investigations of the time required for various mental processes. For three years he studied under (and for part of the time was assistant to) Wilhelm Wundt in the world's first psychological laboratory at the University of Leipzig. After taking his Ph.D. in 1888, Cattell was an assistant in Galton's Anthropometric Laboratory; he also lectured and collected psychological test data in the United States and at Cambridge. In 1890, two years after he became professor of

JAMES McKEEN CATTELL (1860–1944)

Using the model of Galton's Anthropometric Laboratory but with numerous innovations, Cattell inaugurated systematic psychological testing at the University of Pennsylvania (1888) and at Columbia University (1891).

psychology* at the University of Pennsylvania, Cattell gave the following rationale for psychological testing:

> Psychology cannot attain the certainty and exactness of the physical sciences, unless it rests on a foundation of experiment and measurement. A step in this direction could be made by applying a series of mental tests and measurements to a large number of individuals. The results would be of considerable scientific value in discovering the constancy of mental processes, their interdependence, and their variation under different circumstances. Individuals, besides, would find their tests interesting, and, perhaps, useful in regard to training, mode of life or indication of disease. The scientific and practical value of such tests would be much increased should a uniform system be adopted, so that determinations made at different times and places could be compared and combined.

Interested individuals could take a battery of tests in a laboratory which Cattell established. Here are his descriptions (considerably abridged):

* Cattell was the first individual to have this title. Up to this time, psychologists on university faculties generally had titles in philosophy.

I. *Dynamometer Pressure.* The greatest possible squeeze of the hand may be thought by many to be a purely physiological quantity. It is, however, impossible to separate bodily from mental energy. The squeeze of the hand may be readily made, cannot prove injurious, is dependent on mental conditions, and allows comparison of right- and left-handed power. The experimentee should be shown how to hold the dynamometer in order to obtain the maximum pressure. I allow two trials with each hand (the order being right, left, right, left), and record the maximum pressure of each hand.

II. *Rate of Movement.* The rate of movement has the same psychological bearings as the force of movement. As a general test, I suggest the quickest possible movement of the right hand and arm from rest through 50 cm. An electric current is closed by the first movement of the hand, and broken when the movement through 50 cm. has been completed.

III. *Sensation-Areas.* The distance on the skin by which two points must be separated in order that they may be felt as two is a constant, interesting both to the physiologist and psychologist. Its variation in different parts of the body (from 1 to 68 mm.) was a most important discovery. What the individual variation may be, and what inferences may be drawn from it, cannot be foreseen; but anything which may throw light on the development of the idea of space deserves careful study. Compasses with rounded wooden or rubber tips should be used. The points must be touched simultaneously, and not too hard.

IV. *Pressure Causing Pain.* The point at which pressure causes pain may be an important constant, and in any case it would be valuable in the diagnosis of nervous diseases and in studying abnormal states of consciousness. To determine the pressure causing pain I use an instrument which measures the pressure applied by a tip of hard rubber 5 mm. in radius. I am now determining the pressure causing pain in different parts of the body; for the present series I recommend the center of the forehead. The pressure should be gradually increased, and the maximum read from the indicator. I make two trials and record both.

V. *Least Noticeable Difference in Weight.* The just noticeable sensation and the least noticeable difference in sensation are psychological constants of great interest. I follow Mr. Galton in selecting "sense of effort" or weight. I use small wooden boxes, the standard one weighing 100 gms. and the others 101, 102, up to 110 gms. The standard weight and another (beginning with 105 gms.) being given to the experimentee, he is asked which is the heavier. I allow him about 10 secs. for decision. I record the point at which he is usually right, being careful to note that he is always right with the next heavier weight.

VI. *Reaction-Time for Sound.* The time elapsing before a stimulus calls forth a movement should certainly be included in a series of psychophysical tests: the question to be decided is what stimulus should be chosen. I prefer sound, on it the reaction-time seems to be the shortest and most regular, and the apparatus is most easily arranged. In measuring the reaction-time, I suggest that three valid reactions be taken, and the minimum recorded. Later, the average and mean variation may be calculated.

VII. *Time for Naming Colors.* The time needed to see and name a color may be readily measured for a single color by means of suitable apparatus, but for general use sufficient accuracy may be attained by allowing the experimentee to name ten colors and taking the average. I paste colored papers (red, yellow, green, and blue) 2 cm. square, 1 cm. apart, vertically on a strip of black pasteboard. This I suddenly uncover and start a chronoscope, which I stop when the ten colors have been named. I allow two trials (the order of colors being different in each) and record the average time per color in the quickest trial.

VIII. *Bisection of a Fifty-Centimeter Line.* The accuracy with which space and time are judged may be readily tested. I follow Mr. Galton in letting the experimentee divide an ebony rule (3 cm. wide) into two equal parts by means of a movable line, but I recommend 50 cm. in place of 1 ft., as with the latter the error is so small that it is difficult to measure, and the metric system seems preferable. The amount of error in mm. (the distance from the true middle) should be recorded, and whether it is to the right or left. One trial would seem to be sufficient.

IX. *Judgment of Ten Seconds of Time.* This determination is easily made. I strike on the table with the end of a pencil, and again after 10 seconds, and let the experimentee in turn strike when he judges an equal interval to have elapsed. I allow only one trial and record the time, from which the amount and direction of error can be seen.

X. *Number of Letters Repeated on Once Hearing.* Memory and attention may be tested by determining how many letters can be repeated on hearing once. I name distinctly and at the rate of two per second six letters, and if the experimentee can repeat these after me I go on to seven, then eight, etc.; if the six are not correctly repeated after three trials (with different letters), I give five, four, etc. The maximum number of letters which can be grasped and remembered is thus determined. Consonants only should be used in order to avoid syllables.

Cattell also developed a battery of fifty tests to be taken by students in experimental psychology:

Sight

1. Accommodation (short sight, over-sight, and astigmatism).
2. Drawing Purkinje's figures and the blind spot.
3. Acuteness of color vision, including lowest red and highest violet visible.
4. Determination of the field of vision for form and color.
5. Determination of what the experimentee considers a normal red, yellow, green, and blue.
6. Least perceptible light, and least amount of color distinguished from grey.
7. Least noticeable difference in intensity, determined for stimuli of three degrees of brightness.
8. The time a color must work on the retina in order to produce a sensation, the maximum sensation and a given degree of fatigue.
9. Nature and duration of after-images.
10. Measurement of amount of contrast.
11. Accuracy with which distance can be judged with one and with two eyes.
12. Test with stereoscope and for struggle of the two fields of vision.
13. Errors of perception, including bisection of line, drawing of square, etc.
14. Color and arrangement and colors preferred. Shape of figure and of rectangle preferred.

Hearing

15. Least perceptible sound and least noticeable difference in intensity for sounds of three degrees of loudness.
16. Lowest and highest tone audible, least perceptible difference in pitch for C, C′, and C″ and point where intervals and chords (in melody and harmony) are just noticed to be out of tune.
17. Judgment of absolute pitch and of the nature of intervals, chords, and dischords.
18. Number and nature of the overtones which can be heard with and without resonators.
19. Accuracy with which direction and distance of sounds can be judged.
20. Accuracy with which a rhythm can be followed and complexity of rhythm can be grasped.
21. Point at which loudness and shrillness of sound become painful. Point at which beats are the most disagreeable.
22. Sound of nature most agreeable. Musical tone, chord, instrument, and composition preferred.

Taste and Smell

23. Least perceptible amount of cane-sugar, quinine, cooking salt and sulphuric acid, and determination of the parts of the mouth with which they are tasted.
24. Least perceptible amount of camphor and bromine.
25. Tastes and smells found to be peculiarly agreeable and disagreeable.

Touch and Temperature

26. Least noticeable pressure for different parts of the body.
27. Least noticeable difference in pressure, with weights of 10, 100, and 1000 gms.
28. Measurement of sensation-areas in different parts of the body.
29. Accuracy with which the amount and direction of the motion of a point over the skin can be judged.
30. Least noticeable difference in temperature.
31. Mapping out of heat, cold, and pressure spots on the skin.
32. The point at which pressure and heat and cold cause pain.

Sense of Effort and Movement

33. Least noticeable difference in weight, in lifting weights of 10, 100, and 1000 gms.
34. Force of squeeze of hands, pressure with thumb and forefinger and pull as archer.
35. Maximum and normal rate of movement.
36. Accuracy with which the force, extent, and rate of active and passive movements can be judged.

Mental Time

37. The time stimuli must work on the ear and eye in order to call forth sensations.
38. The reaction-time for sound, light, pressure, and electrical stimulation.
39. The perception-time for colors, objects, letters, and words.
40. The time of naming colors, objects, letters, and words.
41. The time it takes to remember and to come to a decision.
42. The time of mental association.
43. The effects of attention, practice, and fatigue on mental times.

Mental Intensity

44. Results of different methods used for determining the least noticeable difference in sensation.
45. Mental intensity as a function of mental time.

Mental Extensity

46. Number of impressions which can be simultaneously perceived.
47. Number of successive impressions which can be correctly repeated, and number of times a larger number of successive impressions must be heard or seen in order that they may be correctly repeated.
48. The rate at which a simple sensation fades from memory.
49. Accuracy with which intervals of time can be remembered.
50. The correlation of mental time, intensity, and extensity.

In a comment on this battery published as an addendum to Cattell's article, Galton drew attention to the need of an outside criterion by which to evaluate a testing procedure, and also, perhaps, hinted at the appraisal techniques of modern clinical psychologists:

> One of the most important objects of measurement is hardly if at all alluded to here and should be emphasized. It is to obtain a general knowledge of the capacities of man by sinking shafts, as it were, at a few critical points. In order to ascertain the best points for the purpose, the sets of measures should be compared with an independent estimate of the man's powers. We thus may learn which of the measures are the most instructive. The sort of estimate I have in view and which I would suggest should be noted is something of this kind—"mobile, eager energetic; well shaped; successful at games requiring good eye and hand; sensitive; good at music and drawing." Such estimates would be far from worthless when made after only a few minutes' talk; they ought to be exact when made of students who have been for months and years under observation. I lately saw a considerable collection of such estimates, made by a medical man for a special purpose. They were singularly searching and they hit off, with a few well chosen epithets, a very great variety of different characters. I could not induce the medical man to consent to the publication of specimens of his excellent analyses, nor even of fancy* specimens. Even these would have sufficed to show that if psychologists seriously practiced the art of briefly describing characters, they might raise that art to a higher level.

Cattell's lists clearly indicate the state of the art of mental testing half a dozen years after Galton opened his Anthropometric Laboratory. Tests were largely of sensory and motor functions, with related measures of perception, association, and memory beginning to appear. Simple apparatus was usually involved, and scoring tended to be in terms of physical units, such as time, distance, pitch, temperature, and force. Most of the measures were obviously related to the experimental psychology of the day, which emphasized the study of sensation, reaction time, and discrimination.

FURTHER AMERICAN DEVELOPMENTS

In 1891 Cattell went to Columbia University, where he founded the Psychological Laboratory, and soon he inaugurated a battery of physical and mentals tests (many of which were on his 1890 list) which

* Had Galton been an American he probably would have used the word "imaginary" or "fictitious" instead of "fancy."

were given each year to approximately fifty freshmen in Columbia College, as well as to some young women at Barnard and to some college seniors. Preliminary results, consisting chiefly of means and variabilities, were published in collaboration with Livingston Farrand (who later became president of Cornell University) (Cattell and Farrand, 1896). Five years later Clark Wissler (1901) published an elaborate statistical analysis (the first ever of this magnitude) reporting the interrelationships among the mental tests as well as their relationships with college grades. Results were disappointing. The laboratory mental tests had low intercorrelations. While class grades showed appreciable correlations with grades in other courses, no dependable relationships were discovered between class grades and laboratory tests. A promising start in mental measurement apparently had failed.

Meanwhile, both in the United States and abroad, psychological testing continued to develop. In the laboratories that were founded at Harvard, Yale, Clark, Chicago, Wisconsin, and other universities, provision was made for the testing of individual differences. Joseph Jastrow, who established the laboratory at Wisconsin, also conducted psychological testing open to the public at the Columbian Exposition in Chicago in 1893. Two years later the American Psychological Association appointed a committee to study the feasibility of cooperation among the various psychological laboratories in the collection of mental and physical statistics. Cattell and Jastrow were members of this com-

LIGHTNER WITMER (1867–1956)

Founder of the first Psychological Clinic (University of Pennsylvania, 1896).

mittee, as was Lightner Witmer (Cattell's first student but a Leipzig Ph.D.), who in 1896 established at the University of Pennsylvania the first Psychological Clinic, in which the techniques of the psychological laboratory were used in the study of handicapped children.

At Columbia, Cattell had a number of students who later distinguished themselves in measurement. In 1898 E. L. Thorndike (1874–1949) wrote a dissertation in which he reported the use of mazes and puzzles to measure the intelligence of cats (Thorndike, 1898), and Cattell advised him to apply the method to children. Some of Thorn-

EDWARD L. THORNDIKE (1874–1949)

Author of the first book in psychological statistics (1904). Thorndike originated methods for assessing handwriting, clerical aptitude, and reading comprehension. His students pioneered in the measurement of interests, mechanical abilities, and educational achievement.

dike's many achievements in psychological testing will be mentioned later, along with contributions of others of Cattell's students, including R. S. Woodworth (1869–1962), F. L. Wells (1884–1964), and E. K. Strong, Jr. (1884–1963).

KRAEPELIN AND HIS STUDENTS

While little in the measurement of individual differences emanated directly from Wundt's laboratory, several important early developments in psychological testing took place in Germany, where the work of

Cattell was well known. Emil Kraepelin (1856–1926), a psychiatrist who had been one of Wundt's first pupils, put forth (Kraepelin, 1894) a program of applying the methods of psychology to psychopathology.

EMIL KRAEPELIN (1856–1926)

With several associates, Kraepelin inaugurated comparative psychological testing of the sane and insane (1894).

Pointing out that the causes of mental illness vary with the individual, he proposed a comprehensive system of comparative testing of the sane and the insane that would consider personal characteristics, such as mental ability, trainability, memory, sensitivity, fatigability, ability to recover from fatigue, depth of sleep, and distractibility. His plan involved performance of mental tasks of everyday life, such as adding numbers, on different days and under different conditions, so as to lead to measures of the degree of the characteristic under study. He recognized the need for standard procedures in testing and the need to examine each case a sufficient number of times so that chance variation would be excluded, and so that the existence of true personal differences would be established.

Kraepelin's student, Axel Oehrn (1896) used a number of tests in an intensive study of ten individuals, one of whom was Kraepelin himself. Oehrn's tests were intended to measure psychological functions: perception, memory, association, and motor skills. The specific tasks included counting letters singly and in groups of three, memory span for digits and for nonsense syllables, adding single digits to obtain sums of 100, writing from dictation, and reading aloud.

Oehrn's objective was to obtain normative data on healthy individuals, with whom the mentally ill could be compared. Oehrn actually tested a few patients, but it remained for subsequent pupils of Kraepelin to explore differences in measurable performance between the sane and the insane. Thus, Adolf Gross (1899) sought differences in handwriting and Joseph Reis (1899) explored differences in tasks such as addition; color naming; reading digits, letters, and words; and classifying nouns as depicting either living or nonliving objects. The experiences in testing undoubtedly gave the investigators some insight into mental abnormality, but results were often disappointing, as Cron and Kraepelin (1899) readily admitted.

THE COMPLETION TECHNIQUE

A major breakthrough in testing technique was achieved by Hermann Ebbinghaus (1850–1909), who was searching for an exact and reliable method of measuring mental fatigue in school children. He

HERMANN EBBINGHAUS (1850–1909)

Originator of the completion test for the measurement of intelligence (1896).

decided that true intellectual performance consists of making "combinations," that is, producing wholes which have value and meaning over and above that which is apparent in the sensed situation. He looked for a way to measure the ability of an individual to interrelate, correct, and add to impressions so as to reach a meaningful "combination." His solution was what is now called the "completion" test (Ebbinghaus, 1896). He developed passages of text with words and parts of words omitted and with each omission indicated by a line, as in the following selection from the German version of *Gulliver's Travels*.

Gullivers Reisen

Nach langer Wand——— ————in dem fremden Lande
fühlte ich ——— so schwach, dass ich ——— ———
Ohn———nahe war. Bis ——— Tode ———mattet
s——— ich ins Gras nieder und ——— bald ein, fester
als ———mals in ——— ——— Leben. Als ich
erw——— ———, war der Tag längst ——— ———
brochen; die S——— ———strahlen schienen ———
ganz unerträglich ins ——— ———, da ich auf ———
Rücken ———. U.s.w.

The pupil's task was to fill in as many blanks as possible in the five-minute time limit. Ebbinghaus pointed out the ease with which one could obtain numerical scores by which individuals could be compared as to their intellectual ability.

In somewhat the same way that Leif Ericson anticipated Columbus in the discovery of America, Ebbinghaus anticipated the invention of the group test of intelligence two decades later. His tests were printed on the inside of a folded sheet; on the outside the student wrote name, grade, place, and age. At a signal to begin, the student opened the folder and began to work. He closed it when the signal to stop was given. Whole classes were tested simultaneously. The material was planned to be long enough to occupy each student for five minutes. Ebbinghaus reported that only four times in several thousand cases did a student reach the end of the text without omission of syllables.

While several investigators used the completion technique, including L. M. Terman (1906) in his doctoral research on "Genius and Stupidity" in 1905, and Binet in the first intelligence scale, the practical importance of the group method of administering a psychological test (as contrasted with ordinary classroom examinations) was not recognized. Later, Ebbinghaus' test became the inspiration for Healy's pictorial completion test (1919) and, in modified format, an important component of numerous standardized group measures of intelligence.

The time from Galton's early work in the 1880's to 1905 might be considered the "laboratory period" in mental measurement. A piece of apparatus, say a device for measuring reaction time, might serve both in an experiment seeking a general psychological principle and in another study as a means of measuring person-to-person variability. Characteristically, the same investigators, Cattell as one example, Jastrow as another, published papers on both types of research. Several psychologists, including Gilbert (1894) at Yale, Seashore (1901) at Iowa, and Bagley (1901) at Wisconsin, attempted to relate test results to the estimated intelligence of school children, generally with inconclusive results. Specialized studies began to appear, such as Andrews' (1904) summary of auditory tests, Kuhlmann's (1904) work on the mentally retarded, Thompson's (1903) study of sex differences, and Woodworth's (1910) study of race differences at the World's Fair of 1904 in St. Louis. A few years later, Whipple (1910) published an encyclopedic presentation of testing devices, with extensive bibliographies and summaries of results.

All during the period there was search, explicit or implicit, for a means to measure "intellect," often conceived as the sum of psychological processes, such as sensation, attention, perception, association, and memory.

2

INVENTION OF
THE INDIVIDUAL SCALES

A new period in the history of psychometrics began about 1904 with important discoveries by Binet in France and Spearman in England. We shall consider the French contributions first.

DEVELOPMENTS IN FRANCE

Alfred Binet (1857–1911), whose father and grandfather were physicians and whose mother was an artist, took a degree in law at the age of twenty-one. He then began medical studies; but at Salpêtrière, the mental hospital where Charcot did his clinical teaching, Binet soon became interested primarily in psychopathology and psychology. His early publications were on personality changes, hypnotism, the psychic life of microorganisms, and the psychology of reasoning. His dissertation for the degree of Docteur ès Sciences was on the nervous system of insects. In 1892 he began to work at the Laboratory of Physiological Psychology at the Sorbonne and two years later became its director, a position he was to hold for the rest of his life.

With young children as subjects he began a long series of experimental studies which touched on many of the topics of psychology: memory, movements, sensation, perception, illusions, suggestibility, attention, comprehension, and aesthetic judgment. He searched for relationships between head measurements and behavior and investigated

ALFRED BINET (1857–1911)

Author (with T. Simon) of the first intelligence scale (1905).
Originator of the concept of mental age. Founder and editor of
L'Année Psychologique in which early studies of individual
differences were published.

graphology as a possible means of discovering information about individuals. He devised ways of measuring functions such as memory for words and sentences, and the perception of length, amount, number, and color, and he related the individual differences he found to age and grade placement. The definition of intelligence was a recurrent theme in his articles (many of which were published in *L'Année Psychologique*, a journal which he founded and edited), and in 1890 he had this to say (Binet, 1890b): "In the narrow sense of the word, that which we call intelligence consists of two chief phases: first, to perceive the outside world, and then to reinstate the perceptions in memory, to rework them and to think about them."

BINET'S STUDY OF
INDIVIDUAL DIFFERENCES

With one of his early collaborators, Victor Henri, who had studied with Wundt, Binet (Binet and Henri, 1896) reviewed German and American work on individual differences and pointed out that while elementary psychological processes such as reaction time can be measured with great precision, it is more important to measure the higher psychological processes, in which individual differences are greater. Binet and Henri mentioned the possibility of using mental tests to study races, children, the mentally ill, and criminals. They proposed a battery of tests of complex processes, including several which eventually appeared in intelligence scales: memory for designs, making up sentences to

Fig. 41. — Modèle de dessin montré à travers l'obturateur.

DESIGN WHICH BINET USED IN AN EXPERIMENTAL STUDY (BINET, 1900). The same design became the stimulus in a test item a few years later.

include specified words, and indicating how two concepts are alike and how they are different.

A technique that Binet eventually used in the selection of tests to form a scale of intelligence evolved gradually and first became explicit in connection with memory span. Jacobs (1887) found that the number of digits or letters which a child could remember after two oral presentations increased somewhat with age and also with rank in class. Galton, using Jacobs' method, found memory span more variable but definitely lower in idiots than in normal children. In 1894, Bourdon published a systematic study of memory span in 104 boys, ranging in age from six to twenty years. He discovered that the series most effective in measuring individual differences in this age range were six to eight words. He noted that memory span increased more or less regularly from eight to fourteen years, with only slight increases thereafter. He also found a definite relationship between his tests and brightness as judged by teachers who used three categories: "intelligent," "average," and "unintelligent." Later, Binet and Henri (1895a, 1895b) found only a small overall increment from seven to twelve years of age in memory span for words, but a regular increase in the number of ideas recalled from sentences. For psychometric purposes Bourdon's experimental design was the more advanced, in that he used a wider range of ages and included intelligence ratings as a criterion.

In the decade that followed, Binet published frequently on individual differences, including a series of eighteen studies on physical and physiological measures undertaken in collaboration with N. Vaschide (1898). In a discussion of the problem of measuring characteristics such as keenness of intellect and soundness of judgment, he pointed out that an a priori system of measurement probably would not fit the great variety of expressions of intelligence, and that, accordingly, a satisfactory system must be built on the basis of experience.

At this time Binet was still thinking of measurement by specific tests rather than by a group of diverse tests, the method which was adopted several years later. He classified each test as one of two types: a constant task, with the result obtained taken as the measure; or a variable task, which could be adjusted to the ability of the subject, thus yielding a measurement. As an example of the first type he cited showing a table with fourteen familiar objects to children for five seconds and then requiring them to list all the objects they could remember. As an example of the second type he cited the memory span experiment, in which a subject is given a set of lengthening series of digits, the measurement being the longest series the individual can repeat without error. Binet pointed out, however, that the numbers obtained from tests were classifications rather than true amounts, since we do not know that the difference between a memory span of eight digits and one of seven is the same as the difference between a memory span of seven digits and one of six. He thereby anticipated present day discussions of the meanings of numbers used in psychological measurement.

Binet and Vaschide (1897) proposed a ranking method of describing the relationship between two variables. After individuals were ranked on the two variables, differences in rank without regard to sign were averaged to obtain a "coefficient de différence." This could be taken as a description of the degree of relationship between the variables, with zero representing perfect direct relationship, an intermediate value representing no relationship, and a high value indicating an inverse relationship. Several years later better rank correlation methods were developed by Spearman.

THE INFLUENCE OF BLIN AND DAMAYE

As noted earlier, the first decade of Binet's work on individual differences followed the prevailing practice of considering only one test at a time. In 1903, however, he published L'Étude Expérimentale *de l'Intelligence,* a study in which he applied twenty tests of complex processes to describe and differentiate the personalities of his two daughters, Armande and Marguerite.

About this time Binet was impressed by the work of two psychiatrists, Dr. Blin (1902) and his pupil, Dr. Damaye, who had attempted to improve the diagnosis of mental retardation by a series of assessments in each of twenty areas. The areas, each of which was assigned a score of from 0 to 5, included appearance; spoken language; responses to sets of questions on topics such as self, parents, and age; knowledge of parts of the body; obedience to simple commands; naming common objects; ideas of time and place; ability to read, write, and perform simple arithmetical computations; and, finally, attitude during the examination. For each of these areas there were three sets of questions graded according to difficulty: one set for children less than 10 years of age, one for those between 10 and 13, and one for those over 13. Normal children almost always received a score of 100 on the questions appropriate for their age; retarded children had scores between 0 and 100.

Binet approved the basic idea of a set form of examination ("affected neither by the bad humor nor the bad digestion of the examiner") covering a wide range of topics. He noted also that it had actually been applied to 250 subjects at Vaucluse, a home and training institution for retarded children. Nevertheless, he criticized the scale as subjective in content, format, and scoring. He objected particularly to items reflecting formal education and to questions which could be answered "yes" or "no." Such answers, he said, do not demonstrate whether the question itself has been well understood. It is better, he went on to say, to use a format which will force the child to develop his thought (if he has one).

Despite these criticisms, Binet and his collaborator Simon (1905a) hailed the work of Blin and Damaye as the first attempt to apply scientific method to the diagnosis of mental retardation, and they soon adapted their idea of a total score, based on a number of tasks, to reflect gradations in intelligence.

THE RESOLUTION SUBMITTED TO THE GOVERNMENT

Binet was a very active member and an early president of the Société Libre pour l'Étude de l'Enfant, which held monthly meetings in Paris beginning about 1900. It included school teachers, school administrators, lawyers, professors, physicians, and public officials concerned with education. It was at Binet's suggestion that the society organized a number of interdisciplinary "commissions" or working groups, each to study and report on a specific area of investigation, such as individual aptitudes, moral sentiments, memory, and abnormal children. Binet himself was the president of the group on abnormal children, which, among other activities, prepared a resolution for submission to the government suggesting that "abnormal children, who are not responsive to the usual methods of instruction and whose place is neither in a custodial institution nor in the elementary school, be given a medico-psychological examination and, if a place is available, be taught by a special educational organization" (Binet, 1904). The group left open the controversial question as to whether there should be special instruction in asylums, or whether special schools or special classes in the regular schools should be set up.

Subsequently, in October, 1904, the minister of public instruction appointed a special commission (an ad hoc committee) to make recommendations that would assure abnormal children the benefits of instruction. The president of this commission was Leon Bourgeois, then a senator and formerly a minister of public instruction, whose distinguished career in public service was to continue through World War I. Members of the commission included educators, physicians, scientists, government administrators, and, naturally, Binet.

Actually, there were already in existence special schools for the retarded in the institutions accepting abnormal children, of which the oldest, founded in 1859, was at Salpêtrière. What Binet and his associates had in mind was a wider solution. In a number of sessions, the commission made recommendations about types of establishments, conditions of admission, teaching personnel, and teaching methods. It decided (Binet and Simon, 1905a) that "no child suspected of retardation would be dropped from a regular school and put in a special school without having taken a pedagogical and medical examination showing that his mental state was such that he could not profit, at least moderately, from the teaching in the regular school."

COMPARISON OF METHODS OF DIAGNOSING RETARDATION

Binet assumed the task of studying methods of diagnosing retardation, and, in collaboration with Simon (Binet and Simon, 1905b), compared three methods of differentiating normal and retarded children: a medical examination as it might be made by a physician; an educational examination based on school achievement and other evidence of learning; and a new procedure which they called the psychological method. This method was, in fact, the world's first successful intelligence scale. The date was 1905.

As described by Binet and Simon, the medical method covered hereditary and familial factors; rate of development as shown in teething, walking, and speaking; and various anatomical and physiological signs of inferiority. They regarded this approach as applicable in only a limited number of cases, and as indicating *possible* retardation.

Diagnosis by the educational method included measurement not only of the results of instruction in the ordinary school subjects (arithmetic, grammar, history, geography), but also of everyday information acquired by conversation, reading the newspaper, and general observation, as exemplified in a list of thirty sample questions covering orientation in time and space, family, money, and common objects, activities, and events. Binet and Simon pointed out that this method samples memory, which is only indirectly related to intelligence, and that it does not sample judgment directly. They regarded it as frequently applicable, except with very young children, identifying cases of *probable* retardation.

As contrasted with the medical and educational methods, the psychological method, said Binet and Simon, was almost always applicable, identifying retarded individuals with *near certainty*. Binet and Simon detailed their evidence (1905c). From various sources, but chiefly from Binet's earlier work, they had developed a series of thirty tests which were simple, quick, and convenient to administer and which yielded precise results. The tests were varied in content, depended little on prior instruction, kept the subject in contact with the examiner, and related chiefly to judgment.

The investigators described in detail results with 50 normal children, 10 at each of the following ages: 3, 5, 7, 9, and 11. They also tried out the tests with 26 institutionalized children at Salpêtrière, with varying degrees of retardation, as well as with school children judged to be below normal in intellectual ability. Comparison with results with normal youngsters provided a means by which mentally defective children, idiots, imbeciles, and morons, could be described in terms of years of retardation.

THE 1905 INTELLIGENCE SCALE

The 1905 scale was hardly novel in content, since Binet had studied many of the thirty tests in one form or another in investigations going back a number of years. The test involving comparison of the

A PICTURE USED BY BINET IN THE 1905 SCALE. Binet
was a pioneer in the use of pictures as test stimuli. Here the
child was instructed to find and point out the window, the
mother, big sister, the little girl, the cat, the broom, etc.

lengths of lines (Binet, 1890a), for example, had been used in 1890,
and the task involving copying a Greek design (still in use in the current
form of the Binet tests) had been reported in 1900. As stated earlier,
the development of a scale of measures had been suggested by Blin
(1902), and the method of evaluating tests by administering them to
children of different ages and to groups of normal and abnormal
children had been reported by Binet five years earlier (Binet, 1900).

What was novel was a new combination of existing elements.
Binet and Simon had developed the first modern psychological test,
consisting of separate items, chosen systematically in relation to difficulty level and outside criteria (age and judged intelligence), and
published with careful instructions for administration and interpretation.
What had been a "test" now became a subtest or item of a scale which
as a totality yielded a composite measurement of a complex function.
Later, psychologists were to develop formal statistical techniques for
the assessment of item difficulty and of relationships between items
and outside criteria, and Binet himself, in 1908, developed more explicitly the concept of mental age as a way of expressing measured
intelligence. In 1905, after years of patient research, capped by a few
months of intensified and systematic work occasioned by his membership on the ministerial commission, Binet presented to the world an
instrument which was not only useful in its immediate purpose of
diagnosing objectively various degrees of mental retardation but became,
through refinement and further development, the prototype of all
subsequent mental scales.

Even in content Binet did well. With minor modifications, items proposed in 1905 were found useful in his own revisions and in revisions by other psychologists. Among the 1905 subtests that appear with little change in the third Stanford-Binet (Terman and Merrill, 1960) are identifying parts of the body, obeying simple commands, picture vocabulary, repeating sequences of digits, memory for sentences, finding the similarity between two things, comprehension or finding reasons,* paper cutting (in which the subject makes a drawing to show how a paper which is cut while folded would look when it is unfolded), differences between abstract words, and a modification of the Ebbinghaus completion test.

THE 1908 SCALE

The 1905 scale was tried out in Belgium by Decroly and Degand (1906) and, in translation, by Goddard (1908) in the United States. More important, however, were the innovations embodied in a revised intelligence scale which Binet and Simon published in 1908.

HENRY H. GODDARD (1866–1957)

Introduced Binet testing in the United States (1908); participated in the development of the Army psychological tests (1917).

* For example, "Lorsqu'on a été frappé par un camarade, sans qu'il le fît exprès, que faut-il faire?"

A DRAWING USED BY BINET IN THE 1908 SCALE.
With this picture, Binet noted the level of response: enumeration (three year level), description (seven year level), or interpretation (twelve year level).

The new instrument, like the 1905 scale, comprised a series of situations or tasks set by the examiner in which, it was hoped, the child would exhibit problem solving, judgment, and the ability to learn, rather than ready-made responses previously acquired. New tests which were introduced at this time (and which are used today in much the original form) included: naming as many words as possible in a limited amount of time, naming the days of the week, reconstructing scrambled sentences,* copying a diamond, and executing three commands (putting an object on a chair, opening a door, and then bringing a box). Another innovation was a test for the detection of absurdities or incongruities, which, in various forms, has come to be an important item type in intelligence testing. Some material which has continued to be used in individual tests of intelligence for children was expanded and improved: repetition of sentences, and finding differences between pairs of concepts.

Instead of thirty tests arranged in approximate order of difficulty, there were now fifty-eight tests arranged in age groups, from age 3 through age 13. Certain material was actually presented to the child only once but counted as items on two or more levels. For example, if the response of the child to a picture was enumeration of objects, success was at the 3-year level; if description, then success was at the 7-year level; while interpretation gave credit at the 12-year level.

Careful instructions were presented for administration and scoring of all the tests, and for finding the mental age. In the 1908 revision,

* For example, "Sommes la pour de heure bonne nous campagne partis."

mental age was in integral units of one year and was defined as the age level at which the subject passed all tests but one, with added credit of one year for passing five tests above that level and added credit of two years for passing ten additional tests. Fractional credit assigned in computing mental age was to be a refinement of the 1911 revision.

Binet and Simon did not regard the new scale as a perfected instrument, but they pointed out that items had been included only after careful try-out. They suggested that future test developers might succeed in more rigorously discarding tests influenced by formal instruction. They also rejected a mechanistic view of intelligence testing, stating:

> In spite of appearances, the method is not automatic, like a scale in a railroad station, on which it is necessary only to step for the machine to emit a ticket with our weight printed on it. Neither is it a routine operation, and we predict that the hurried physician who wants to have it applied by nurses will have his vexations. The results of our examination have no value if separated from all comment; they must be interpreted.

The scale was applied to 303 children in the Paris schools, ranging from age 3 through age 12, each within two months of his birthday. A more or less symmetrical distribution was found: 12 were two years retarded, 44 one year retarded, 103 had mental ages corresponding to their chronological ages, 42 were one year advanced, and 2 were two years advanced. In all cases children who were doing exceptionally well in school also did exceptionally well on the tests.

It was in 1908 that Binet saw more clearly than ever the implications of his success in measuring mental ability, of both bright and retarded children. He proposed that the method be used not only for adapting educational programs to individual differences in ability but also as an aid in determining the responsibility of criminals and in classifying army inductees. He planned to develop educational achievement tests which would permit evaluation both of teaching methods and of teachers, and aptitude tests to be used for vocational guidance. Later, in a discussion of military applications of psychological testing (Binet, 1911b), he pointed out that group tests of intelligence were feasible. Unfortunately, Binet's ambitious program was not to be accomplished in his lifetime.

Following publication of the 1908 scale, the Binet procedure was widely adopted both in Europe and in the United States. Since then, many changes have been made in the assignment of particular tests to various age levels; better items have been developed and less satisfactory items have been discarded; and large and well selected groups of sub-

PICTURE FROM THE 1908 BINET SCALE. Employed by
Binet only to gauge mental level, this picture is somewhat similar
to those used thirty years later in the assessment of personality.

jects have been used in standardizing new editions of the Binet type
of intelligence scale. Nevertheless, the method remains basically as
Binet described it in 1908.

In 1911, the year in which he died, Binet published a number of
modifications: adjustment of the age levels of certain tests, the use of
five tests on each age level, replacement of the tests for age 11 and
age 13 with tests for age 15 and for adults (thus extending the range
of the scale), and the use of fractions in reporting mental age. He also
reported a series of studies: on the relationship between school success
and mental level; on the effect of retesting on scores; on the methods
used by teachers in judging intelligence; and on the relationship
between socioeconomic status and measured intelligence.

As a procedure deeply rooted in the techniques of the psychological
laboratory, Binet and his collaborators firmly established intelligence
testing in a format which continues to this day: a well trained examiner
testing a single child. In one place or another Binet discussed many of
the problems connected with individual testing: the need for the examiner to establish rapport with the child, the need to start the testing
at a level at which the child is likely to succeed and to terminate it
before the child is unduly fatigued, the need to maintain the child's
interest, and the use of accurate records in evaluating results.

STERN'S MENTAL QUOTIENT

A major development in connection with the interpretation of
results of mental testing was made by a German psychologist, William
Stern (1911), who pointed out that retardation of a certain amount,

say three years, had different meaning at different ages. Accordingly, Stern suggested that mental age divided by the chronological age be regarded as a "mental quotient," a measure which he found to be relatively constant during the period of mental growth. With various

WILLIAM STERN (1871–1938)

Developed the concept of the Intelligence Quotient.

refinements, including the elimination of the decimal point and methods to insure a uniform mean and standard deviation for each age, the "mental quotient" has become the intelligence quotient or I.Q. in common usage today.

In connection with *L'Année Psychologique,* Binet was an indefatigable reviewer of the English and American psychological literature. Accordingly, he had considerable knowledge of the statistical methods that were taking shape during the two decades he was working on problems of individual differences. Nevertheless, Binet used statistics very sparingly, and it was Charles Spearman (1863–1945) who utilized correlational concepts in formulating a number of principles that have become important parts of psychological test theory.

SPEARMAN AND THE CONCEPT OF RELIABILITY

As a young man Spearman spent a number of years in the British army, much of the time in India. When he was in his middle thirties he went to Leipzig to take his Ph.D. degree under Wilhelm Wundt, founder of the first psychological laboratory. Spearman's principal endeavor was experimental psychology—which he had approached through an interest in philosophy—but he also found time to study physiology and to read the works of Galton and the English statisticians, Pearson and Yule.

CHARLES SPEARMAN (1863–1945)

Originator of the concept of test reliability (1904). His researches in mental organization led to the development of factor analysis.

Spearman was in Germany from 1897 to 1907, except for two additional years of military service in Guernsey and England during the Boer War. It was during this second period of military service that, inspired by Galton's *Inquiries into Human Faculty and its Development*, he collected data on pupils in a village school in Hampshire, which were reported in two important papers published in 1904, "The Proof and Measurement of Association between Two Things" (Spearman, 1904a) and " 'General Intelligence,' Objectively Determined and Measured" (Spearman, 1904b). The first paper introduced the "correction for attenuation" and eventually led to the development of the concept of test reliability; the second presented the core of Spearman's "two-factor" theory of intelligence, and eventually led to the development of methods for locating a general factor underlying a group of tests (this in turn stimulated Thurstone and others to develop multiple factor methods in current use).

Spearman's distinguished academic career was at University College of the University of London, where he was a reader in experimental psychology, beginning in 1907. He was elected to a professorship four years later, and became Chairman of the Department of Psychology when it was separated from the Department of Philosophy in 1928.

While Spearman apparently did not use the term "reliability coefficient" until 1907, he clearly used the underlying concept in his discussions of attenuation (1904a, 1904b). "Suppose," he said, "three balls to be rolled along a well-kept lawn; then the various distances they will go will be almost perfectly correlated to the various forces with which they were impelled. But let these balls be cast with the same inequalities of force down a rough mountainside; then the respective distances eventually attained will have but faint correspondence to the respective original momenta." Irregularities in the mountainous terrain, then, would greatly reduce the correlation between force and distance. In general, the true relationship between any pair of variables, expressed as $\hat{r}_{xy}$, is attenuated by the presence of error in the observed correlation, r_{xy}.

To ascertain the amount of this attenuation and thereby discover the true correlation, Spearman suggested that the investigator make two or more independent series of observations of both x and y and he gave the following formula to be used as the correction for attenuation:

$$\hat{r}_{xy} = \frac{r_{xy}}{\sqrt{r_{xx'} r_{yy'}}}$$

in which r_{xy} is the mean of the correlations obtained from all possible combinations of an x series with a y series, and $r_{xx'}$ and $r_{yy'}$ are the average correlations between the independent x series and y series, respectively.

The formula in current use differs only in that r_{xy} is generally regarded as a single determination of the observed correlation between the two variables and that $r_{xx'}$ and $r_{yy'}$ are estimates of the reliabilities of x and y, determined either through the correlations of independent series of observations, as originally suggested by Spearman, or by methods developed after 1904 by Spearman and others.

Spearman pointed out that many of the investigations of tests reported previously yielded inconclusive or erroneous results because of the failure to take errors of observations into account by either reducing them in the testing situation or, when appropriate, eliminating their effect by correcting the correlations for attenuation. Wissler (1901) had reported that the average intercorrelation of the tests administered by Cattell to Columbia students was only .09 and that their average correlation with intelligence (as estimated from class grades) was .06. Spearman (1910) commented:

> Perhaps the chief source of the lowness of the correlations will be found in the following circumstances, namely: that the subjects were examined three at a time, each being managed by some "student or officer of the department"; that no less than twenty-two different tests were carried out, many of the most difficult character, besides measuring the length and breadth of each reagent's head; that during the leisure moments afforded him in the course of these tests the observing "student or officer of the department" had to note in writing the contour of the reagent's forehead, the character of his hair, the nature of his complexion, the color of his eyes, the shape of his nose, the description of his ears, of his lips, of his hands, of his fingers, of his face and of his head—and that this whole procedure is considered to be satisfactorily completed in forty-five minutes.

Spearman also criticized severely a study by Pearson, who, with government assistance, had been collecting data on the physical and mental characteristics of brothers. In 1901 Pearson published correlations on 800 to 1000 pairs of brothers for seven physical traits, such as stature, eye color, and health, with a mean correlation of .5171; and for ratings by teachers on seven mental traits, such as intelligence, vivacity, and shyness, with a mean correlation of .5214. Judging the mean correlations to be equal, Pearson concluded that mental characteristics in man were inherited in precisely the same manner as physical traits.

Spearman pointed out that there undoubtedly was much more observational error in the ratings of mental characteristics, which could only be estimated, than in the reports of the physical characteristics, which could be measured accurately or at least described precisely. Accordingly, had the correlations been corrected for attenuation, the results would have favored the inheritance of mental traits. On the other hand, he pointed out, the correlations of the mental characteristics were hopelessly distorted because pairs of brothers would have had much the same home and school influences, hence they should show greater similarity. He noted further that with various influences making the correlations inaccurate there was no point in presenting correlations as though they were exact to four decimal places.

The importance of the discovery of the attenuation phenomenon was quickly appreciated by Cattell and other test workers. Psychologists now had at least a partial explanation for the unimpressive results of testing prior to 1904, as well as suggestions on how more useful data might be accumulated and evaluated. They became better aware both of the need for accuracy in collecting scores and of a method that is sometimes useful in estimating what relationships would be found were the measurements perfectly consistent.

In 1907, in an article by Krueger and Spearman, the term reliability coefficient* was introduced to denote a correlation reflecting the consistency of a set of measurements. In 1910 Spearman and his pupil, William Brown, published in separate articles in the same journal a formula for estimating the reliability of a test when lengthened n times. If $r_{xx'}$ is the reliability of the lengthened instrument, and $r_{aa'}$ is the reliability of a device of unit length, then

$$r_{xx'} = \frac{nr_{aa'}}{1 + (n - 1)r_{aa'}}$$

Spearman stated that one way of estimating reliability would be to divide a set of observations into two subsets, one consisting of the odd-numbered items, the other the even-numbered items. Consider, for example, a situation in which the correlation between two such subsets is .50. Then n is 2 and the reliability of the set as a whole would be:

$$r_{xx'} = \frac{2r_{aa'}}{1 + r_{aa'}} = \frac{1.00}{1.50} = .67$$

This formula, known as the Spearman-Brown "prophecy" formula, remains an important means of estimating the reliability of a psychological instrument. The specific technique of dividing items into two subsets which can be considered equivalent is now known as the "split-half" technique.

A further contribution to reliability theory was made by Abelson, working under Spearman's direction. Abelson (1911) demonstrated mathematically that the correlation of observed scores with true scores was $\sqrt{r_{xx'}}$, the square root of the reliability coefficient. Subsequently, $\sqrt{r_{xx'}}$ was christened the "index of reliability," and it is taken as the upper limit of the correlation of an observed variable with any other variable.

Abelson also pointed out that tests of the kind he had been using, which were somewhat similar to those used by Binet, were untrust-

* In German the term is Zuverlässigkeitskoeffizient.

worthy* when used alone. However, he demonstrated theoretically and practically that independent items which in themselves are not very useful may be pooled to yield highly trustworthy results. This was, of course, a restatement of Binet's position—but it was now amply buttressed by theory originating largely with Spearman. It remains a central principle in the construction of psychological tests.

SPEARMAN'S THEORY OF INTELLIGENCE

For more than forty years, beginning in 1904, Spearman's chief attention was given to developing and substantiating a theory of general intelligence. His theory involved:

1. Rejection of the faculty psychology which the experimental psychologists had inherited from the mental philosophers;
2. A statement about the nature of intelligence from which could be deduced types of tests that would measure it; and
3. Mathematical procedures that could be used to support or reject the theory.

Early psychological testing, including that of Galton, Cattell, and Binet, had been oriented in large part toward measuring isolated mental faculties, such as observation, attention, memory, imagination, and reasoning. While Binet came to realize that attention was a better indication of intelligence than sensory acuity, and that tests involving judgment were more useful than tests based on memory, he had not stated as explicitly as Spearman a concept of general intelligence.

Based in part on observations going back to the village school but also on subsequent studies by pupils, associates, and himself, Spearman conceived of a general intellectual factor, which he called g, manifesting itself in varying degrees in a *hierarchy* of mental activities. He stated that two kinds of cognitive abilities had the highest saturations with g: eduction of relations, that is, determining the relationship between two or more stimuli or ideas; and eduction of correlates, that is, with an idea and a relationship stated, finding a second idea correlative with the first.

Even simple sensory discrimination, Spearman decided, involves some g; more g is to be found in activities of intermediate complexity,

* In 1911 the term "validity," indicating the predictiveness of a test, had not yet been introduced. Tests which we would call "valid" were regarded as "trust-worthy" or as "having diagnostic value."

such as arithmetic computation; and the greatest saturation of g is in complicated mental actions. The traditional "faculties" vary internally with respect to the amount of g—reproductive memory has low saturation; problem solving based on memory has high saturation. Similarly, controlled imagination, as in invention, entails much g; uncontrolled imagination, as in free association, very little.

On the basis of his correlational analyses, which seemed to indicate a common factor in various mental tasks, Spearman advocated what Binet actually used beginning in 1905—measurement of intelligence by pooling the results of a wide variety of tests. Spearman's theory that intelligence involves primarily the discovery of relationships and the eduction of correlates helped to explain the special usefulness of certain items appearing in the first Binet scale (and still used), notably the Ebbinghaus completion test, finding similarities and differences between concepts, and making a drawing to show what a paper folded and cut in the child's presence would look like when unfolded.

When Cyril Burt (1911) developed the verbal analogy* as a measure of intelligence, Spearman recognized it as an excellent example of a task involving both eduction of relations and eduction of correlates.

SIR CYRIL BURT (BORN 1883)

Pioneer in applied psychological testing; inventor of the verbal analogy (1910); editor of the *British Journal of Statistical Psychology*.

---

* For example, "Prince is to Princess as King is to _____."

Since 1911, the analogy has become a major component of tests of mental ability, appearing in a wide range of difficulty levels and in various formats, many of them nonverbal.

Spearman recognized that if g were present in varying degrees in different measures and if g alone accounted for the test intercorrelations, then the coefficients themselves could be arranged in a *hierarchy*, diminishing from left to right and from top to bottom, as illustrated below:

HYPOTHETICAL HIERARCHY OF r's

Test	A	B	C	D	E
A		.63	.45	.27	.09
B	.63		.35	.21	.07
C	.45*	.35		.15*	.05
D	.27	.21	.15		.03
E	.09*	.07	.05	.03*	

* These r's form a tetrad.

Other statistical consequences of the presence of a single underlying common factor were discovered:

1. Column to column correlations are perfect;
2. Coefficients in any column are proportional to those in any other; and
3. "Tetrads," formed by taking any four coefficients that form a rectangle and subtracting the product of the pair in the lower left and upper right corners from the product of the other two, must equal zero. (An example involving the four starred coefficients in the table: $.45 \times .03 - .09 \times .15 = .00$)

Spearman did not recognize the problem as one to be solved in terms of matrix algebra, as Thurstone was to do three decades later. Nevertheless, his criteria were correct, and he was the first to use correlation coefficients to indicate the structure of human characteristics underlying test results. He noted that observed matrices of correlations might differ from the hierarchical arrangement for a number of reasons, including unreliability of the measures, fluctuation of r's from sample to sample, and the presence of factors other than g in some but not all of the measures.

In this connection, Spearman hypothesized the existence of various specific or s factors. Some of these were so narrow that they appeared in only one test; such an s factor would have no direct influence upon the correlations of the variable. On the other hand, a broad *s*, called a group factor, might be present in a number of measures and would cause marked distortion of the underlying hierarchy.

Spearman cared little for the practical applications of measurement; he was primarily interested in the psychological test as an instrument in the development of a science of mental life. Cyril Burt, an early associate, was more of a leader in applied psychometrics. He prepared an English version of the Binet scale (Burt, 1921), developed new instruments, conducted testing programs, and contributed to test theory. Spearman's factor methods inspired both controversy and research. In Great Britain, Burt and Godfrey Thomson made important contributions to methods for finding the factors underlying mental tests. In the United States, Holtzinger and Harman continued and extended the Spearman approach, while Kelley, Hotelling, and especially Thurstone were leaders in formulating multiple factor analysis in which a general factor need not be posited.

LEWIS M. TERMAN AND THE STANFORD-BINET

Some of the American contributions to psychometrics in the early decades of the twentieth century results from the continuation of the Galton-Cattell tradition; others were inspired by the Binet breakthrough. Translations and adaptations of the 1905 and 1908 Binet scales were made and put into use, first by Goddard (1908, 1910), whose scales were republished with comments by Whipple (1910) in a comprehensive survey of psychological tests. Other versions of the 1908 scale were developed by Kuhlmann and Wallin, while a "point scale," involving reduction of the amount of material, rearrangement by type of material, and the use of a scoring system involving differential weighting of items and varying credit for different degrees of performance, was published by Yerkes, Bridges, and Hardwick in 1915 and revised and extended by Yerkes and Foster eight years later. The scale with the widest acceptance, however, turned out to be the Stanford Revision of the Binet-Simon Scale, published originally in 1916 by L. M. Terman and revised by Terman and Merrill in 1937 and again in 1960.

Terman's doctoral dissertation, inspired partly by *L'Étude Expérimentale de l'Intelligence*, was planned and executed before the 1905 Binet scale was published. Terman applied tests intended to measure inventiveness and imagination, logical processes, mathematical ability, language, interpretation of fables, learning to play chess, memory, and

 LEWIS M. TERMAN (1877–1956)

Author of the Stanford Revision of the Binet-Simon Intelligence
Scale (1916); co-author of the Army Alpha and the Stanford
Achievement Tests.

motor ability to seven "bright" and seven "stupid" boys selected as
extreme cases from approximately 500 boys with ages fairly close to 11
years. Most of the tests were original, but the completion test was based
on the work of Ebbinghaus, a test of interpretation of fables came from
E. J. Swift, and the following ball-and-field problem (used with some
revision in the 1916 and 1937 Stanford-Binet scales) came from C. F.
Hodge (Terman, 1906):

> A ball is lost in a round field. The grass is so tall that you
> can see only ten feet on each side of you. Show what path you
> would take in looking for the ball.

(The subject was given a pencil and a piece of paper with a circle
representing the field.)

The "Ingenuity Test," used on three levels of the 1960 revision,
first appeared as:

> A mother sent her boy to the river to get four pints of
> water. She gave him only two vessels, one holding three pints,
> the other five pints. The boy must bring exactly four pints, no
> more, no less. How shall he measure it?

A test of making change was developed at this time, with several problems like the following: "How much money should I receive if I buy an article that costs 35 cents and I give the clerk 50 cents?" Binet, to whom Terman sent a copy of his monograph, used change making in the 1908 scale, and it appears on the nine-year level of the current Stanford-Binet.

While Terman found that mental tests differentiated "bright" boys from "stupid" boys, he discontinued research on the measurement of intelligence until after his appointment to the faculty of Stanford University in 1910. Using the 1911 Binet as the source for somewhat over half the items, Terman produced the Stanford-Binet, which became, for several decades at least, the standard instrument for measuring intelligence.

The new scale was based on comprehensive, systematic research. As a first step, data on individual tests given by various workers were tabulated, including per cent passing the test at each age. Next, the Binet material and forty additional tests were prepared for tryout with 905 normal children between the ages of 5 and 14, all within two months of a birthday. In addition, results of testing some 1400 other cases, including 200 defective and superior children and 400 adults, were considered in making the revision. Half a year was spent in training the examiners, another half year in testing. To insure a high degree of uniformity, all records were scored by Terman himself.

To the concept of mental age, introduced by Binet, was added the concept of the intelligence quotient or I.Q., defined as the ratio of mental age to chronological age (multiplied by 100 to remove decimals, and with 16 as the maximum chronological age to be used as a divisor). Stern's mental quotient thus was rechristened and put to use.

During the development of the scale, tests were moved from one age level to another and scoring standards were adjusted until the median mental age of unselected children at each age coincided with the median chronological age, thus assuring a median quotient of 100. In addition, children at each age level were divided into groups: those with I.Q.s of 110 or more, those with I.Q.s between 90 and 109, and those below 90. The percentage of passes on each test at or near the age level was determined for each of the three groups. Items showing a higher percentage of passes for the higher I.Q. groups were chosen. This item selection method, accordingly, involved internal consistency, the correlation between each item and the scale as a whole. Variants of this method are still used in developing tests measuring a single homogeneous function.

The new scale included 90 items: 6 at each age level from three through ten, 8 at age twelve; 6 at "average adult," 6 at "superior adult," and 16 alternates to be used as substitutes when a regular test was contraindicated for some reason. Of the 54 tests in Binet's 1911 series, 3 were eliminated, 4 were shifted up one or two years, 25 were shifted down from one to six years, and 19 were left in the positions assigned by Binet. Although the scale was in the model provided by Binet, it represented much new material and complete restandardization. Of the 36 new tests, 27 came from Terman's work, five were adaptations of early Binet material, one on form discrimination (choosing from simple forms one that matches a sample) had been developed by Kuhlmann, a test of arithmetic reasoning had been adapted from Bonser (1910), while writing in code and a form board test were taken from the work of Healy and Fernald (1911).

With the publication of the Stanford-Binet in 1916, earlier translations and revisions were largely supplanted, and intelligence testing became firmly established in American schools and psychological clinics.

THE DEVELOPMENT OF PERFORMANCE SCALES

Despite the great utility of the new measuring devices, it was recognized that results were not necessarily dependable when they were administered to children who did not speak English as their native language, or who were deaf or had speech defects. As early as the 1904 World's Fair in St. Louis, Woodworth (1910) had used a form board and other performance tests in his study of race differences. To test

SEGUIN'S FORM BOARD. Developed originally as a training device, this form board has been a part of several performance scales for measuring intelligence.

immigrants at Ellis Island for possible mental defect, Knox (1914) had developed a series of tests requiring imitation and other action but no language responses. The Healy and Fernald tests (1911) were developed for use as supplements to the regular scales when children who spoke a foreign language or who had handicaps of various kinds were examined in the Chicago Juvenile Psychopathic Institute. One of the most useful of these tests was a nonverbal application of the concept behind the Ebbinghaus completion test, involving selection of appropriate pieces to complete a picture.

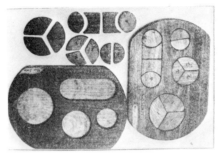

THE CASUIST FORM BOARD. More complex than the Seguin, this board was developed by Knox as a part of his Ellis Island Scale (1914). It became a part of several subsequent performance scales.

The first formal scale to include performance tests, in clinical use in the United States for a number of years, was published by Pintner and Paterson in 1917. Of the fifteen tests, eight were form boards and wooden puzzle boards of various types, five involved completing or assembling parts to form a picture or a human figure ("manikin test") or a face ("feature profile," developed by Knox). Another test devised by Knox, requiring the subject to imitate a pattern tapped out on a set of cubes, was included as was the digit-symbol substitution test originated by Woodworth and Wells (1911). The manikin test and two of the form boards were original. The most venerable of the tests was the form board devised as a training device for retarded children by Edouard Seguin (1812–1880), who was born in France but lived in the United States for more than thirty years. It had been used as a test by Norsworthy and by Goddard, and subsequently standardized by Sylvester (1913). All the other tests in the series were restandardized by Pintner and Paterson, who provided four types of norms: an age scale; a method involving finding a mental age for each test administered and then the median of these mental ages; a point scale; and percentile norms for each age group. Of the four methods the median mental age seems to have had widest acceptance. Most of the tests were scored in

EDOUARD SEGUIN (1812–1880)

Primarily concerned with the treatment of mental retardation through training of the muscles and the senses, Seguin invented the form board as an instructional device.

RUDOLF PINTNER (1884–1942)

Co-author of the Pintner–Paterson Scale of Performance Tests (1917).

terms of both errors and time, with a time limit beyond which the test was considered a failure.

In the years just before and after the Pintner-Paterson scale was published, three important performance tests were invented and standardized: the Porteus Maze, the Kohs Block Design test, and the Goodenough Draw-a-Man test.

DONALD G. PATERSON (1892–1961)

With Pintner, author of a performance scale standardized for clinical use (1917); co-director of the Minnesota Mechanical Ability investigation.

The Porteus, first published in 1915 (Porteus, 1915), consists of a graded series of printed mazes through which the subject is to thread his way with a pencil. Whenever a cul-de-sac is entered or a line crossed, that particular maze is considered failed and is taken away. The mazes were developed as a supplement to the Binet in diagnosing mental retardation, and there is evidence that maze scores reflect prudence, foresight, and the power of sustained attention. Modified and extended somewhat from time to time, the Porteus Maze was included in the 1930 Arthur Point Scale of Performance Tests. It has also had considerable independent use in psychological clinics and has been a durable research instrument (Porteus, 1959).

The Kohs Block Design test also was included in the Arthur scale and, in various modifications, has been a part of almost every American performance scale since its original publication in 1920 (Kohs, 1920).

KNOX'S FEATURE PROFILE TEST (1914)

The subject is provided with a set of identical cubes painted a different color on each side. The task of the subject is to reproduce with the blocks a set of patterns presented on a series of cards, one at a time. A wide range of ability can be measured nonverbally with tasks which most subjects find interesting.

In the Goodenough test, published in 1926, a child's drawing of a man is graded for presence or absence of details, such as parts of the body and articles of clothing. Artistic merit is ignored. As a psychometric device it has been a useful supplement to other scales. Good-

STANLEY D. PORTEUS (BORN 1883)

Inventor of the Porteus Maze Test (1914) on which he has carried out more than five decades of research.

SAMUEL C. KOHS (BORN 1890)

Author of the Kohs Block Design Test (1920).

FLORENCE L. GOODENOUGH (1886–1959)

Author of the Draw-a-Man Test (1926).

enough noted that abnormal children often made highly individualistic drawings. In fact, it has become common practice to regard samples of behavior involving drawings of people and things as indicating internal motivational and emotional processes. Consequently, as will be mentioned again later, the Draw-a-Man test has evolved into what is often called a "projective" device.

3

THE DEVELOPMENT
OF GROUP TESTS

The group test of intelligence took shape gradually. For generations academic examinations had been given to classes of difference sizes, and, as noted earlier, Ebbinghaus had used a printed group test to measure intelligence. With the success of the Binet scale, measurement of mental abilities by a device that could be administered simultaneously to large numbers of subjects was a logical next step. Whipple (1910) commented as follows:

> Most mental tests may be administered either to individuals or to groups. Both methods have advantages and disadvantages. The group method has, of course, the particular merit of economy of time; a class of 50 or 100 children may take a test in less than a fiftieth or a hundredth of the time needed to administer the same test individually. Again, in certain comparative studies, e.g., of the effects of a week's vacation upon the mental efficiency of school children, it becomes imperative that all S's should take the tests at the same time. On the other hand, there are almost sure to be some S's in every group that, for one reason or another, fail to follow instructions or to execute the test to the best of their ability. The individual method allows E to detect these cases, and in general, by the exercise of personal supervision, to gain, as noted above, valuable information concerning S's attitude toward the test.

EARLY GROUP TESTS

Pyle (1913) published age norms for a battery of group mental tests which had been described in Whipple's Manual, including several association tests from the Woodworth-Wells series. The battery was intended to be used diagnostically. Memory was tested in two ways: by a logical memory test in which ideas were counted in the child's written reproduction of a story, and by memory span for words. Quickness of learning was tested by two substitution tests, digit-symbol and symbol-digit. Tests intended to measure inventiveness, imagination, and speed of association were also included. Actually, Pyle's series followed the Galton-Cattell approach of attempting to measure different mental faculties rather than measuring general mental ability, as in the Binet-Spearman tradition.

Pintner (1917) published a report showing how he had modified Pyle's approach so as to measure general intelligence. Using the five tests from Pyle that seemed to have the highest correlations with general intelligence, together with a test involving "cancellation" of the letter *a* whenever it appeared in a body of type and two tests of following simple directions from the Woodworth-Wells series, Pintner calculated mental ages from each test and used the median of these

ARTHUR S. OTIS (1886–1964)

Otis provided the model for the 1917 Army group test of intelligence. Completely objective scoring and the multiple choice item were important innovations.

mental ages, which served as a good approximation of the mental age as found with the Yerkes-Bridges Point Scale. At age 14 the relationship was not satisfactory, but for ages 8 through 13, correlations ranged from .74 to .95, demonstrating that group mental testing was possible.

While the group test was evolving, it did not yet exist in modern form. The device of presenting a question and two or more alternative answers from among which the subject was to choose the correct response was known but not yet in general use. Both Thorndike and Thurstone had arranged material so that items could be scored by key, but it was A. S. Otis, working with Terman at Stanford University, who first developed a group intelligence test which included various types of material and which could be scored completely objectively. Otis had not yet published his test when the United States entered World War I in 1917, but it became the prototype of the Army Alpha, the instrument with which large-scale testing was inaugurated.

THE U.S. ARMY TESTING PROGRAM

When war came, Robert M. Yerkes was president of the American Psychological Association. He immediately took energetic steps to dis-

ROBERT M. YERKES (1876–1956)

Ranking psychologist in the U.S. Army in World War I, Yerkes provided the leadership that resulted in rapid advances in psychometrics and in popularization of group testing.

cover and implement ways in which psychology could be of service in the national effort. Committees of psychologists were organized, of which the most important (at least in the history of psychometrics) was one on the psychological examination of recruits. Yerkes was chairman of this committee as well as of what became its parent group, the Psychology Committee of the National Research Council.

When Yerkes assembled the committee on the examination of recruits late in May, 1917, at the Vineland Training School, its membership included: W. V. Bingham, who had been pioneering as head

WALTER V. BINGHAM (1880–1952)

Member of the committee that designed Examination *a*, predecessor of the Army Alpha. Designer of the Army Trade tests, and architect of the classification system of the U. S. Army.

of the Division of Applied Psychology at the Carnegie Institute of Technology; H. H. Goddard, who had introduced the Binet scale to the United States; T. H. Haines, psychologist and psychiatrist; L. M. Terman, who had just completed the Stanford Revision of the Binet and who brought with him group test material and related statistics which Otis had made available to the committee; F. L. Wells, clinical psychologist and joint author of the Woodworth-Wells association tests; and G. M. Whipple, who had produced the most comprehensive survey of psychological tests published up to that time.

In a discussion of possible contributions of psychology to military efficiency, the committee decided that psychological tests offered the best possibility for practical service. When the relative merits of brief

COMMITTEE ON THE EXAMINATION OF RECRUITS, VINELAND, (1917). Front row: E. A. Doll, H. H. Goddard, T. H. Haines. Back row: F. L. Wells, G. M. Whipple, R. M. Yerkes (Chairman), W. V. Bingham, L. M. Terman. (Doll was not a member of the committee, but was commissioned later to serve in the Army program.) (Photograph from the collection of H. H. Goddard; in the Archives of the History of American Psychology.)

individual tests, which had been suggested by Yerkes, and group tests requiring a longer time were considered, the committee agreed unanimously that an effort should be made to test all recruits. If this were done by interview and individual examination, the tests would be so brief that their reliability would be questionable. Furthermore, as pointed out in the official report (Yerkes, 1919), "the briefer the examination and the more it depended upon expert estimate by a clinical psychologist, the more difficult it would be to secure uniformity of method and interpretation of results." The decision was made to develop a group test of intelligence.

CRITERIA FOR THE DEVELOPMENT OF THE NEW GROUP TEST

In deciding on the material to be included the following criteria were adopted:

1. Adaptability for group use.
2. Correlation with measures of intelligence known to be valid.

3. Measurement of a wide range of ability.
4. Objectivity of scoring, preferably by stencils.
5. Rapidity of scoring.
6. Possibility of many alternate forms so as to discourage coaching.
7. Unfavorableness to malingering.
8. Unfavorableness to cheating.
9. Independence of school training.
10. Minimum of writing in making responses.
11. Material intrinsically interesting.
12. Economy of time.

In seven working days, the committee considered many types of material, selected ten as subtests for development, constructed enough items of each type of material for ten different forms, and prepared

RECRUITS TAKING EXAMINATION *a* AT CAMP LEE, 1917. The administrator is Ben D. Wood. (U.S. Signal Corps photo number 11–SC–386 in the National Archives.)

one form for printing and experimental administration.* The committee adjourned to try out the test with various subjects—somewhat

* Instructions and sample items from Examination *a*, which was the preliminary Army test, are given in the Appendix.

less than 500 altogether. Experimental subjects included inmates of a school for the retarded, a psychopathic hospital, and a reformatory; aviation recruits; and men in an officers' training camp. Terman was able to test 60 high school pupils and 43 prisoners who had already been tested with the Stanford-Binet. The new test, together with an abbreviated Binet scale, was also given to 114 Marines at a Navy yard.

When the committee reassembled, total score was found to correlate .87 with the Stanford-Binet and .81 with the abbreviated Binet, both outside measures of recognized validity. Instructions and items were edited, time limits revised, and scoring formulas developed to yield high correlations of total score with the Binet and of subtests with total score. In addition, items within each subtest were rearranged approximately in order of difficulty, and four alternate forms with items selected by chance from the item pools were sent to the printer.

By August a statistical unit under the direction of Thorndike at Columbia University had analyzed the results of the revised test administered to 3,129 soldiers and 372 inmates of institutions for mental defectives. Thorndike pronounced the new instrument the best group test ever devised. He found that it yielded good distributions of scores and differentiated various levels of intelligence, such as mentally retarded adults, normals, and men who gain success in a profession or as a military officer. He reported correlations of approximately .50 with ratings by superior officers and of .67 with amount of schooling.

THE ARMY ALPHA

Four months later, as the result of further experience with recruits and officers, Examination *a* was revised once more and now became the celebrated Army Alpha. Of the ten subtests in the preliminary instrument, some had been found to yield low correlations with other measures, some gave too high a proportion of zero or perfect scores, some contained ambiguous items, and some were improperly weighted. It was also believed that the test was less reliable for high-grade than for average men and that its reliability at the lower extreme was also doubtful. Accordingly, various adjustments were made.

Table 1 summarizes the composition of the Army Alpha, the number of items in each of the eight subtests, time limits, original sources, and committee members primarily responsible for assembling materials in the original planning sessions at Vineland.

The Army testing program, which was under the direction of Yerkes throughout World War I, was the first large-scale use of in-

TABLE 1

Sources of Army Alpha Material

Test	Number of Items	Time Limit (Min.)	Original Sources	Army Material Assembled By
1. Oral Directions	12	**	Abelson (1911), Otis, Woodworth-Wells (1911)	Whipple
2. Arithmetical Reasoning	20	5		Bingham
3. Practical Judgment	16	1½	Binet, Bonser (1910)	Haines, Goddard
4. Synonym-Antonym	40	1½	Otis	Terman
5. Disarranged Sentences	24	2	Binet (Otis adaptation)	Haines, Goddard
6. Number Series Completion	20	3	Rogers (1918)	Wells
7. Analogies	40	3	Otis, Bingham, Thurstone	Terman
8. Information	40	4	Wells, Bingham, Whipple	Wells

** 5 to 25 seconds per item.

telligence tests. Some 1,726,966 men were examined, of which at least
1,250,000 were tested with one of the five forms of the Army Alpha.
It had good acceptance by the military establishment, which used the
results in making important personnel decisions. Unprecedented numbers of psychologists were involved, including a large proportion of the
leaders in American psychology. When the war ended, there were
examining units in 35 camps, staffed with 120 officers and 350 enlisted
men. (One of the enlisted men was David Wechsler, whose intelligence
scale, first published two decades later, was to challenge both the
Stanford-Binet and the nonverbal performance measures.)

HANDSCORING EXAMINATION *a* AT CAMP LEE, 1917.
A distinctive feature of the group examination designed for Army
use was that it could be scored by the use of objective keys.
(U. S. Signal Corps photo number 11–SC–388 in the National
Archives.)

   The program was sophisticated in that much attention was given
to basic psychometric issues, including the reliability and validity of the
measurements. Hundreds of correlation coefficients were computed, including a number of multiple correlations, being used for the first time
in connection with psychological test results. Karl Pearson prepared a
graph of the relationship between the Army Alpha and the Army Beta,
a nonverbal group test designed for use with illiterates and recruits
speaking foreign languages.

THE IMPACT OF THE ARMY PROGRAM

The greatest impact of the Army program was on psychologists and their concept of the role of psychology in society. Before World War I psychology was largely an academic discipline; thereafter it became more and more a profession. The conspicuous success of the program engendered confidence in measuring new variables and applying the results not only in schools and child guidance clinics but also in vocational counseling and in the selection of industrial personnel. None of this was really new: books on applied psychology were beginning to appear; Hugo Münsterberg before his death in 1916 had been conducting experimental investigations in various fields of applied psychology; a Division of Applied Psychology had been active at the Carnegie Institute of Technology since 1915; and the first number of the *Journal of Applied Psychology* was issued the month before the United States

HUGO MÜNSTERBERG (1863–1916)

Pioneer in psychological testing in industry.

entered the war. But the group test as developed in the Army was a more flexible tool than had hitherto existed, and psychologists now saw that their methods for measuring individual differences could be refined and extended into new areas.

In 1918 Otis published the group test which had been the principal model for the Army Alpha; a year later Thorndike produced an intelligence test for high school graduates, standardized on college freshmen. After that the flood began, with new group intelligence tests appearing each year. A large proportion were for the primary grades, but some were intended for advanced students or for use in business. Many were verbal and contained item types similar to those in the Army Alpha; others followed the Army Beta in consisting largely of pictures and diagrams and requiring no language responses. A new principle, apparently introduced by Otis in 1922, was the "self-administering" test, consisting of items of different types arranged in a mixed order and with an overall time limit of perhaps 30 minutes for the whole test instead of separately timed subtests.

It was generally recognized that tests administered to a number of individuals at the same time did not permit the kind of clinical observation that is possible during examinations of the Binet type, nor were the results as reliable. While findings from group intelligence tests administered to children have often been interpreted in terms of mental age and I.Q., it has come to be considered good practice to regard such scores as tentative and to retest all doubtful cases using one of the individual scales.

It is appropriate at this point to describe early developments in the measurement of academic achievement, special aptitudes, interests, and personality characteristics. Early attempts at objective educational measurement date back to the time of Binet and earlier, and there were beginnings in the measurement of special aptitudes and of interests before the Army program. Nevertheless, it was the widespread appreciation of the Army program which greatly stimulated the making and standardizing of a wide variety of new measures and accelerated their application.

THE MEASUREMENT OF PROFICIENCY IN SCHOOL SUBJECTS

As pointed out earlier, university oral examinations originated in medieval times, and by the late sixteenth century written examinations had been introduced in elementary schools. In such examinations, however, students were compared either with some sort of subjective standard or with other students in the same group. In 1864 it was reported (Chadwick, 1864) that the Rev. George Fisher of Greenwich,

England, had collected specimens of academic performance in various areas, including writing, spelling, mathematics, and grammar and composition, and had arranged them in a permanent "Scale Book" with assigned values from 1, the best, to 5, the poorest. Intermediate values were indicated by fractions. Work by any student could then be graded by direct comparison with a set of specimens arranged in order of merit, thus providing a fixed standard of grading in each of the subject matter areas.

RICE'S SURVEYS OF
EDUCATIONAL ACHIEVEMENT

More influential on the development of standardized educational tests in the United States was the work of Joseph M. Rice, who in the late 1880's gave up his medical practice in order to investigate means of increasing the efficiency of learning in the schools. After training in psychology and pedagogy at Jena and Leipzig, Dr. Rice studied a

JOSEPH MAYER RICE (1857–1934)

Pioneer in progressive education, educational research, and educational measurement. His comparative studies of spelling (1897), arithmetic (1902), and language (1903) greatly influenced the work of Thorndike and later investigators.

number of school systems and reported his findings in a series of articles in *The Forum*, a magazine of which he eventually became editor. As a first step toward placing elementary education on a scientific basis, he proposed to determine what results might reasonably be expected at the end of a given period of instruction.

Rice (1897) reported the results of measuring the spelling achievement of some 33,000 school children. His first method, involving a standard list of 50 words administered by local school officials, was not satisfactory because of differences in the way the words were pronounced. Later, he tested some 13,000 children personally, using words embodied in sentences and being careful not to include words of which the pronunciation could be a direct clue to the spelling. His analysis of the results led him to conclude that 10 to 15 minutes of daily instruction in spelling was just as effective as 40 or 50 minutes.

Later (1902), he examined 6,000 children with an arithmetic test (eight examples at each level, with some overlapping of problems) and 8,300 children with a test in language (1903). As with the spelling test, he was interested in determining the effects of specific educational programs and of influences such as pupil maturation, rather than in the development of instruments for the evaluation of individuals. The fact that he administered common examinations to large samples of school children and determined mean scores to be expected at different grade levels was an important step toward the development of standardized tests.

THORNDIKE'S INFLUENCE ON ACHIEVEMENT TESTING

The work of Rice evoked much interest on the part of E. L. Thorndike, with the result that for a number of years Teachers College, Columbia University, was the chief center for the development of new measures of educational achievement, many of which were published by Thorndike's students, including C. W. Stone, S. A. Courtis, M. B. Hillegas, B. R. Buckingham, and, later, M. R. Trabue, Clifford Woody, W. S. Gray, and A. I. Gates. L. P. Ayres, another pioneer in educational measurement, was at one time an associate of Thorndike.

Stone (1908), who published his arithmetic tests in 1908, improved on Rice's procedures by separating arithmetical ability into two somewhat independent skills, arithmetical reasoning and fundamentals of arithmetic, as had already been suggested by Thorndike. Stone also arranged his problems in order of difficulty on the basis of preliminary trials, established time limits, provided standard instructions for administration, and used correlation coefficients in evaluating the results.

Thorndike had been critical of Rice's scoring procedure, which was simply the number of items answered correctly. Stone's method was to give more weight in the final score to the more difficult items and less weight to the easier ones.

Another advance in educational measurement came with Thorndike's publication of a handwriting scale (or "graphometer") in 1910. Thorndike used the judgments of competent judges as the basis for selecting key handwriting specimens and assigning them scale values; for children in grades 5 through 8, for whom the scale was intended,

FROM THE THORNDIKE HANDWRITING SCALE.
(1910). Specimens to be scored were compared with a series of samples, each with a predetermined scale value.

these ranged from 7 (low) to 17 (high). A few specimens outside the 7-to-17 range were also included, and at each scale point alternate specimens in different styles of writing were provided whenever possible.

To use a handwriting scale, a sample to be evaluated is matched as closely as possible with one of the key specimens, and the numerical scale value of the key specimen becomes the score indicating the merit of the sample.

In developing the scale, Thorndike asked his judges to evaluate 1,000 specimens by placing them in one of eleven groups, each with an assigned numerical value. The median of the judgments of 23 to 55 judges was taken as the numerical value of the specimen. Specimens with values that were very close to integers (7 through 17) became the key specimens of the scale. In this way, differences judged to be equal by the combined opinion of competent judges were considered to constitute equal units on the scale.

In the same article Thorndike published an alternate handwriting scale developed on the Fullerton-Cattell (1892) equal-distance theorem, namely, that differences that are equally often noticed are equal (unless they are always noticed or never noticed). Thorndike was able to select twelve key specimens such that by direct comparison each of eleven of them had been judged by approximately 80 per cent of the judges to be better than the specimen immediately below it in the scale.

In 1912 the Fullerton-Cattell theorem was used by Hillegas (1912) in developing a scale for the measurement of English composition, and since then it has been used not only in various scales measuring educational achievement but also in the development of attitude measures.

About this time Courtis became the first professional educator to make a survey of school achievement in the fashion which Rice had pioneered. This was in the New York City school system. Courtis was, of course, able to use better tests, including the arithmetic test he had published in 1909 and better statistical techniques for summarizing the results. Nevertheless, after much experience with school surveys, Courtis (1925) wrote:

> How great the inefficiency of public education really is few realize in spite of the repeated revelations of survey data. The results of Rice, the pioneer in the modern movement for exact comparative measurement, were received with open disbelief and ridicule; but they have been substantiated by survey after survey the country over. Today there can be no excuse for ignoring the fact that very few children profit as they should from training experience in any single function, and that the range of ability in any one grade is so great that each grade is practically an ungraded group with respect to a single specific ability.

Important spelling scales were published by Buckingham (1915) and Ayres (1915), a language scale using incomplete sentences by Trabue (1916), and a test of the fundamentals of arithmetic by Woody (1916). Thorndike himself worked extensively on reading skills, and published his first measures of reading words and of reading sentences in 1914.

In 1916, the year of publication of the Stanford-Binet, Daniel Starch summarized the state of the art of educational measurement, presenting a wide variety of instruments and pointing out potential uses, including the experimental evaluation of different instructional methods. Thereafter, educational measurement gathered momentum. Achievement tests were developed for all subject matter areas; many tests were sufficiently diagnostic so that they could be used to locate sources of specific disabilities; and comprehensive batteries with a number of tests standardized on the same population came into vogue. Publishers began to distribute tests developed by authors scattered throughout the country. Tests manuals were written to give information on how and why the test was developed, evidence of reliability, methods of administration and scoring, the meaning of norms, and suggested applications.

A great stimulus for the growth of educational measurement was the invention of the multiple-choice item, first used extensively in the Army Alpha. Educational test makers soon discovered that an item consisting of a clearly written stem, followed by four or five alternative answers, of which one is correct, provides a flexible format for the measurement of both knowledge and skill.

Another stimulus was the popularity of the printed test of intelligence. Shortly after the Otis Group Intelligence Scale was published in 1918, an early brochure stated:

> The success of the Otis Scale has been entirely unprecedented in the history of American schoolbook publishing. After the first edition was issued in March it was necessary to put through a second printing in June of a hundred thousand; and in September it was necessary to print a third of a million more. Plans were then laid for a still larger printing in December in order to supply schools examining pupils at the mid-year.

Some idea of the rapidity of the expansion of educational testing in the 1920's can be obtained from *Table* 2, abstracted from Lee (1936). This table covers only tests suitable for use in grades 9 through 12, and it omits prognostic and aptitude measures, rating scales, non-standardized instruments, tests not commercially available, and devices for which copyright dates were not available. During this period, development of achievement tests for the lower grades was also progressing very rapidly.

TABLE 2

Copyright Dates of Standardized Achievement Tests Suitable for Use in Grades 9–12

Subject	Before 1920	1920	1921	1922	1923	1924	1925	1926	1927	1928	1929
English											
Composition	3			1	1		1	1	2	2	1
Language, Grammar	4	1	1	1	6	2	2	2	5	3	1
Literature, Poetry		1	1	1			2	3	2	1	3
Reading, Vocabulary	1	1	4		2		2	1	3	2	1
Spelling	1	1						1			
Speech								2			
Foreign Language											
Latin	3		2	2	4	1	2				
French	1		1				2	2	1	2	2
Spanish	1						1	3	3	2	1
German							1	1	1	1	
Mathematics											
Algebra	1	1							1	1	1
Geometry	1		1						1	1	2
Solid Geometry, Trigonometry						1	1	3		3	
Social Science											
American History		1	1					1	1	1	
European History		1									
World History								1		1	
Civics								2	1	3	
Miscellaneous						2				1	

TABLE 2 (continued)

Copyright Dates of Standardized Achievement Tests Suitable for Use in Grades 9-12

Subject	Before 1920	1920	1921	1922	1923	1924	1925	1926	1927	1928	1929
Science											
General Science					1	1		1			1
Chemistry					1	2			2		2
Physics			1	1				2	1		
Biology	1					3		1		1	3
Botany							1				
Industrial Arts											
Manual Arts									2	3	2
Mechanical Drawing										1	3
Home Economics	1		1		1	2		1	2	2	
Commercial											
Arithmetic and Business						1		1			2
Bookkeeping							1			1	
Shorthand			1	2	1						
Typewriting					1						1
Miscellaneous								1			
Fine Arts											
Music	1					2		1	1		
Art									1		2
Freehand Drawing				1							
Miscellaneous											
Agriculture						4				2	
Health, Personal Education							2	1	2	1	2
Achievement Batteries					1	1			1		1

75

TESTING IN THE COLLEGES

In testing at the college level, Thorndike was again a pioneer. During the war he had modified the first Army test for use with candidates for the School of Military Aeronautics, chiefly by adding more difficult items and new subtests. Later, he shortened this test for use in examining some 10,000 candidates for an Army training program at Columbia University. University authorities were so much impressed with the effectiveness of the instrument that early in 1919 the use of an intelligence test was established as an alternative method of determining admission to regular college classes. For this purpose and for use in other colleges, the Thorndike Intelligence Examination for High School Graduates was developed.

While the test was almost immediately discovered to be highly valid, it was soon suggested that college grades could be made more accurate by the use of objective examinations. Ben D. Wood, a young

BEN D. WOOD (BORN 1894)

Pioneer in the use of objective tests in education. First director of the Cooperative Test Service, he stimulated the invention of the test scoring machine.

veteran of the Army psychological program and a doctoral student under Thorndike, provided technical assistance to the staff of the course in Contemporary Civilization in constructing true-false, completion, and multiple-choice achievement items, the results of which were to be compared with standings on a traditional essay examination.

Findings as presented by Wood (1923) showed objective examinations to be more reliable statistically than the essay tests. Instructors liked the "new examinations" because they were far more comprehensive than earlier methods of testing and because the chance of personal favoritism influencing scores was practically eliminated. Good results in other subjects, including physics, government, and zoology, firmly established the use of objective tests at the college level.

These first tests were tailored to specific courses and were administered as final examinations. Soon Wood was to be a leader in the development of standardized achievement tests for use in higher education, tests with preliminary try-out of items, standard instructions to insure uniform administration and scoring, known reliability, and adequate norms for the interpretation of scores. One of his early endeavors was in connection with the construction of a placement test in French based in part on word counts of widely used textbooks. Later, as director of the Cooperative Test Service of the American Council on Education, he utilized the talents of some of the nation's best test builders in developing a comprehensive array of achievement tests for use in high schools and colleges. By the 1930's objective tests for measuring academic achievement had become firmly established in American education.

THE MEASUREMENT OF INTERESTS

Thorndike published on the measurement of interests as early as 1912, reporting a study in which 100 students ranked their interests in seven subject matter areas when they were in elementary school, in high school, and, finally, in college. Later the students were asked to rank abilities in the same areas for the same three periods. Enough consistency was found to indicate to Thorndike that the topic was worth investigating with improved techniques, stating that a "better method is, of course, to get the measurements of relative interest and relative ability, not from memory, but at the time; and not from individuals' reports alone, but by objective tests."

In 1914 a student of Thorndike's, Truman Lee Kelley (later to make important contributions to statistical methods useful with test data), wrote a doctoral dissertation which involved the development of interest measures which were then correlated with achievement in English, history, and mathematics.* Kelley asked pupils to report magazines (from a list of seventy) that they found most interesting, books

* Kelley's test is included in the Appendix.

TRUMAN L. KELLEY (1884–1961)

Developer of the item type used in many interest tests (1914).
Psychometric theory was advanced by his "Statistical Method"
(1921).

they liked, and activities they thought they would enjoy. He used
judges to establish the probable relevance of various responses to
success in the subject matter areas, with the result that correlations
between interest scores and grades in corresponding subjects ranged
from .26 to .46.

Development of standardized interest inventories was centered for
a time at the Carnegie Institute of Technology, now Carnegie Mellon
University, Pittsburgh. J. B. Miner (1922) developed an interest blank
to help high school students relate their vocational choice to funda-
mental personal interests. Two new features were a list of occupational
activities, among which the pupil was to indicate his first three choices;
and a list of paired contrasting work conditions, in which the more
appealing of each pair was to be checked.

Later, in a seminar on interests conducted in 1919–20 by C. S.
Yoakum (1921), some 1,000 items relating to interests from childhood
through early maturity were constructed. This pool of items was drawn
upon in various subsequent studies.

One part of a "Record of Interests," constructed by Moore (1921),
was a list of occupations selected so as to include equal numbers of
occupations similar to sales and to engineering. When asked to desig-
nate a preference for an alternate occupation, design engineering
students chose occupations such as architect, automobile repairman,

or carpenter; sales engineers chose occupations such as bank cashier, hotel keeper, or lawyer.

In 1921 several members of Yoakum's seminar took part in the construction of what became the prototype of many subsequent interest inventories—the Carnegie Interest Inventory. Part I was a list of occupations; after each one the subject was to encircle L if he would like doing that kind of work, D if he would dislike it, and ? if he had no decided feeling or knew nothing of it. The first four items were as follows:

Actor	L	?	D
Architect	L	?	D
Astronomer	L	?	D
Auctioneer	L	?	D

The second part had to do with likes and dislikes, including categories of people, recreations, magazines, motion picture actors, and activities. For each of these items, the response was to be in one of five categories, as indicated after the following sample items:

Fat men	L!	L	?	D	D!
Golf	L!	L	?	D	D!
National Geographic Magazine	L!	L	?	D	D!
Charlie Chaplin	L!	L	?	D	D!
Telling a story	L!	L	?	D	D!

Ream (1924) developed an empirical key for salesmen by counting only those items on which responses of successful salesmen differed by a certain minimum amount from those of unsuccessful salesmen. The introduction of this empirical procedure was a significant advance in the technique of interest measurement. The same technique was used by Freyd (1922–23), differentiating between men primarily inclined toward social occupations, involving handling and motivating people, and individuals predominantly inclined toward objects and machines.

THE STRONG VOCATIONAL
INTEREST BLANK

E. K. Strong, Jr., a psychologist who was to make the measurement of vocational interests his primary professional endeavor, was on the faculty at Carnegie during this period, but his publications were on job analysis, industrial training, and salesmanship. In 1923 he was appointed to the staff at Stanford. There, jointly with T. L. Kelley, he

EDWARD K. STRONG, JR. (1884–1963)

Author of the Strong Vocational Interest Blank (1927). Subsequent researches on interests spanned 35 years.

supervised the doctoral dissertation of K. M. Cowdery (1926–27) on the differential measurement of interests of lawyers, physicians, and engineers.

Cowdery made several improvements over previous work. He modified the Carnegie interest blank to include items covering 84 occupations, 78 types of people, 34 sports and amusements, 6 kinds of pets, 13 representative kinds of reading, 23 miscellaneous activities, and 25 school subjects. His primary or criterion group of subjects consisted of 105 carefully selected successful professional people: 34 doctors, 37 engineers, and 34 lawyers. The distribution of responses for each item was tabulated separately for each profession, and the correlation found between the item on the one hand and membership or nonmembership in a given profession on the other. Kelley suggested a weighting formula for the items: $r/(1 - r^2)s_i$, in which r is the item validity (found as a phi coefficient between dichotomized item responses and group membership) and s_i is the item standard deviation. While the formula does not take item intercorrelations into account, it yields weights that can be taken as rough approximations to multiple regression coefficients, which theoretically would yield the perfect solution. An even more important innovation was cross-validation of the new scales on new groups of professionals and on control groups of nonprofessionals. This was a check on whether the differentiations made in the original samples turned largely upon dependable differences in responses or involved the capitalization on error variance. Cowdery demonstrated that different professional groups tend to have distinctive response patterns, a fact that continues to be the foundation for the measurement of vocational interests.

Strong (1926) worked at first with Cowdery's blank, increasing the number of occupations studied to eighteen; enlarging the samples; and evaluating results in terms of three letter grades, A (obtained by the most typical 75 per cent of successful individuals in an occupational group), B (obtained by the remaining 25 per cent of the group), and C (with a score more or less outside the distribution for the occupation in question). Each person taking the test could be scored on the key for each of the occupations, yielding a series of scores designed to be useful in vocational guidance. Strong also simplified the calculations for developing item weights, using as his base differences in percentages of individuals in the profession in question and of individuals outside that occupation.

The Strong Vocational Interest Blank, which rapidly found wide acceptance, both for vocational guidance and for research, was first published in 1927. Of the 263 items in the Cowdery inventory, 182 were retained and 81 were discarded. Of the 238 new items, approximately half were in three new sections: order of preference of activities, comparisons of interests, and rating of present abilities and characteristics. The 420 items (slightly reduced in later editions) constituted a comprehensive inventory of interests. For 36 years, until his death in 1963, Strong devoted his energy and talent to the development of empirical keys, using large and well-selected groups of respondents; to studies of reliability and validity and of variation in interests over time; to the development of manuals and devices to aid in the interpretation of results; and to making various improvements in the device itself and in scoring methods. The original instrument eventually became the Vocational Interest Blank for Men, and a companion blank for women was introduced in 1933.

THE KUDER PREFERENCE RECORD

Various individuals developed and published similar interest tests, but none had the broad empirical base or the wide acceptance of the Strong. In 1934, however, G. F. Kuder published the Kuder Preference

Record—Vocational, an instrument which, in various editions, has been widely used and has also stimulated much research. It differs from the Strong in forcing choices within triads of items; thus it compares the

G. FREDERIC KUDER (BORN 1903)

Discoverer (with Marion W. Richardson) of the method of rational equivalence for estimating test reliability (K–R 20). Author of interest measures and editor of *Educational and Psychological Measurement.*

relative strength of interests within the individual, rather than placing chief reliance on empirical comparison of professional groups with men and women in general.

TESTS OF SPECIAL SKILLS AND APTITUDES

As noted earlier, the United States Civil Service Commission began its program of measuring skills and aptitudes required for specific jobs in the 1880's. The Commission developed a number of work sample tests long before professional psychologists were involved in the measurement of vocational proficiency and aptitude. Early in 1917 the Commission began to make contacts with psychologists engaged in psychometric research. Upon request, Thorndike arranged for the Commission to inspect tests which he had constructed for clerical workers of a life insurance company. Shortly after the end of World War I, an experimental administration of the Army Alpha by Yerkes to a group of civil service clerical workers acquainted the Commission with the possibilities of the multiple-choice format for their own examinations. With the appointment of L. J. O'Rourke as director of research in 1922, various new test development and validation procedures were incorporated into the work of the Commission (Filer and O'Rourke, 1922–23).

As early as 1913, Hugo Münsterberg, a pioneer in applied psychology at Harvard University, showed that laboratory measurements of reactions were related to the job performances of streetcar motormen and of telephone switchboard operators. Work on tests to select salesmen was undertaken by Walter Dill Scott and others at Carnegie Institute, but it was the stimulus of war activities that brought about systematic development of vocational tests.

In 1915, H. L. Hollingworth wrote on the theory of vocational testing, pointing out that there were at that time some twenty types of work for which tests had more or less tentatively been tried out. He proposed four classes of vocational tests. The first was the *vocational miniature*, in which the entire job or some important part of it is reproduced by a miniature apparatus such that the task required in the testing situation is essentially the same as that ordinarily facing the worker. In *vocational sampling*, a selection of the tasks generally required of the worker becomes the basis of measurement. In *vocational analogy*, the test does not involve reproduction of the work situation either in whole or in part, but is judged to require identical abilities. As an example he cited a dot-striking test for measuring accuracy of aim and coordination, essential factors in manipulating a switchboard. His fourth class was *empirical tests*, in which some measure is found to have a dependable relationship with job success, even though no reason for the correlation is immediately apparent.

APTITUDE MEASUREMENT
IN WORLD WAR I

Early in 1916 Henry C. Link, working in an arms plant in New Haven, Connecticut, found that a card-sorting test and a cancellation test (from the Woodworth-Wells series) were valid for shell inspectors and that a tapping test was valid for gaugers. Over a period of two years, Link correlated test results with success in various occupational groups, including assemblers, clerks, stenographers, typists, and production machine operators. As reported (Link, 1919), results indicated that a systematic program of (1) job analysis, (2) experimental administration of tests thought to require the same abilities as required

HENRY C. LINK (1889–1952)

In a World War I arms plant, Link developed a systematic
program of using psychological tests for employee selection.

on the job, and (3) correlation of test results with later job success,
could be used to select psychological instruments differentiating between those job applicants likely to be good risks and poor risks.

Within the armed services in World War I (Yerkes, 1919), a
number of studies of special aptitudes were carried out. Raymond
Dodge built a device that was successful both as a selection test and as
a training instrument for naval gun pointers. He also worked out testing
procedures for selecting candidates for the plotting room and the
listener's school, both naval specialties of the time. For the selection of
telegraphers, Thurstone (1919a) developed a "rhythm test" in which
dots and dashes presented auditorily were to be reproduced by the
subjects as written dots and dashes. It had a correlation of .48 with
highest receiving speed attained during the first hundred hours of
practice. Thurstone also systematically compared the specially developed instrument with seven other psychological tests, finding some
useful and others useless for predicting actual performance. In a
multiple correlation against the criterion, the rhythm test was found
to carry most of the weight. In this study Thurstone demonstrated the
technique that is often used in developing a test to predict behavior:
development of one or more instruments believed to measure the ability

LEON L. THURSTONE (1887–1955)

Pioneer in the measurement of vocational aptitudes and of attitudes; founder of multiple factor analysis.

or abilities required by the criterion task; experimental administration to a large group of individuals prior to training; correlation of test results with actual success; and recommendations for revised selection procedures based on empirical findings.

Among the numerous subcommittees of the Psychology Committee of the National Research Council was a committee on the psychological problems of aviation, including the examination of aviation recruits. Several psychophysical tests involving motor coordination and quickness of response were found to be predictive of flying ability (Henmon, 1919). Between the wars this work was continued by medical officers at the School of Aviation Medicine at Randolph Field, who built the prototype of one of the psychomotor tests used extensively for the selection of flying personnel in World War II.

In connection with the examination of aviation recruits, Thorndike found a positive correlation between athletic ability as reported in the application blanks filled out by candidates and subsequent success in flying. This was an early instance of the predictive use of "biographical data," which through the years have been found to have predictive validity for occupations that include life insurance sales and various military specialties.

THE MEASUREMENT OF PROFICIENCY

To assist in the proper placement of recruits, a 1917 Committee on the Classification of Personnel in the Army, of which Bingham was the chairman, developed and standardized an extensive series of trade tests. Material for the tests was sought from skilled mechanics in the trades represented, trade union officials, employment managers, factory superintendents and foremen, the United States Bureau of Labor Statistics, civil service examiners, and Army officers. Essential elements of each job were translated into questions which might be used to test the capacity of the worker. After criticism by experts, an original pool of about 80 of these questions for each trade was reduced to 40 questions; these were then administered to 20 expert workmen, 20 of journeyman grade, 20 apprentices, and 20 men of ordinary intelligence who were novices so far as the trade in question was concerned. The best questions were then selected and standardized so that the final score would indicate the level of skill for the trade (Bingham, 1919).

Before the armistice in 1918, there had been produced 83 oral trade tests, 40 trade tests in picture form, and 30 performance tests, in which the recruit performed essential processes of the trade under standardized conditions of administration and scoring. Among the performance measures were tests for auto mechanic, electrician, sheet metal worker, structural steel worker, and electrical lineman. A number of the tests were put into operational use, and by the time of the armistice some 130,000 recruits had been examined with them.

TESTS IN ART AND MUSIC

An important occasion in the history of aptitude measurement was the publication of *Measures of Musical Talent* by Carl Seashore (1919). The six basic measures, sense of pitch, intensity, time, consonance, tonal memory, and rhythm, resulted from years of laboratory work at the University of Iowa on the psychology of music. Not only did the Seashore Measures tap a new field, they were also notable for being based on careful analyses of the components of a complex skill. They introduced a novel testing medium—sound reproduced from phonograph records. Various printed tests of musical knowledge as well as tests on records somewhat similar to the Seashore have been published since the early 1920's, but the Seashore Measures, revised in 1939, continue to be useful in the identification of potential musical ability.

CARL E. SEASHORE (1866–1949)

Inventor of the Seashore Measures of Musical Talents (1919).

Another innovation in test development procedures came in the 1920's. Several authors, Lewerenz, McAdory, and Meier and Seashore, all used expert judges in the assessment of material to be included in tests of ability and judgment in visual art. Evaluation of test material by qualified judges is often useful when the attribute to be measured lacks an objective criterion. Art tests have had some application both in predicting success in art curricula and in vocational guidance.

TESTS IN BUSINESS OCCUPATIONS

In the measurement of proficiency and aptitude for business occupations there were two more or less independent developments. For use in the schools, achievement tests were developed for commercial subjects, just as they had been for academic studies. A widely used set of objective but unstandardized measures covering memory, spelling, punctuation, grammar, handwriting, filing, tabulating, typing, bookkeeping, and answering letters was published in 1919 by a professional writer (Cody, 1919). More important scientifically was the careful research on clerical aptitude carried on by psychologists.

Another pioneer in the field of measurement of clerical aptitude, after the early work of Thorndike and of Link, was Thurstone (1919b). He developed and administered to over 5,000 office clerks in various companies a "standardized sample office job" requiring 45 to 60 minutes.

The eight parts of the examination included: checking errors in addition and subtraction; finding misspelled words in a section of text; finding and cancelling certain letters; code learning; alphabetizing and writing names; classifying insurance policies; simple problems in arithmetic; and intelligence as measured by matching proverbs. He reported a correlation of .50 between an accuracy score and grade of office work actually performed, while the validity of a speed score obtained from the test was .42.

Other clerical aptitude tests soon yielded good validities against office work criteria. In 1922, Filer and O'Rourke reported a correlation of .70 between the U. S. Civil Service General Clerical examination and efficiency ratings on the job. Two years later, Ruggles (1924) used six tests based on job analysis: checking for sameness; comparing; locating alphabetically; classifying and sorting; tabulation; and arithmetic computation. He found average correlations of .30 or more with supervisors' rankings of efficiency of work.

Perhaps one of the reasons for the early and continued success of clerical testing has been the ease of evoking in the test situation behavior more or less identical with that required on the job. This test behavior is in part tasks (or items) easily scorable for speed and accuracy.

MECHANICAL, MANUAL, AND SPATIAL TESTS

The boundaries marking off mechanical aptitude measures, manual or motor tests, and tests of spatial abilities are by no means clear and definite. Occasionally the nomenclature is confused; sometimes the measured functions overlap. Devices in this area have a common history in that originally all involved apparatus and were administered either to one subject at a time or to small groups of subjects. Later, many of the tests were modified for administration to large groups; and in some cases printed tests were developed to measure functions somewhat similar to those measured originally by apparatus. In practice, the three terms are convenient rubrics for tests that involve little or no language but require overt or implicit manipulation or assembly of objects or shapes.

MECHANICAL TESTS

The distinguishing characteristic of "mechanical" tests is, perhaps, that they tend to involve the manipulation of real-life objects, that is, objects with everyday functions outside the psychometric situation. One of the earliest workers in this area was J. L. Stenquist, who, with Thorndike and Trabue, published in 1915 a study of the results of tests applied to 265 dependent and delinquent children. One of the instruments used in this study was the "Stenquist Test of Mechanical Ability or Construction Test," based on Thorndike's suggestion that the presentation of a disassembled commercial article, such as bicycle bell, to be assembled by the subject, was a promising way of tapping capacities not then measured by printed verbal tests. Stenquist's instrument could be administered to twenty-four children at a time by two examiners. Each child was provided with a box which included seven assembled objects to be used as models, together with all the disassembled parts necessary to duplicate the objects, which included a bolt and nut, a small monkey wrench, a mouse trap, a simple door lock, and special objects made in part from angle irons and screw eyes. Scoring was on the basis of 0 to 10 points for assembly of each of the objects, with an extra point for each minute less than 30 used to complete the series of tasks. For comparative purposes the test was also administered to 432 public school children. (The authors found that dependent children were retarded on the Mechanical Ability Test but less so than on the Binet and the Trabue Completion Test. Both the Stenquist and the Completion Test seemed worthy of further development.)

On the recommendation of Thorndike, a revision of the Stenquist test, with ten objects to be assembled but no models to follow, was used for a time in the Army during World War I as a group test for illiterates and as a special test of mechanical skill. More than 14,000 men were examined with it.

After the war Stenquist developed two alternate series of ten items each for Grades 5 and above, and also an easier series for Grades 3 through 6. He also developed and standardized two picture tests of mechanical aptitude, involving judgments of mechanical relationships and a general knowledge of things mechanical—their principles, operations, and use. He reported correlations as high as .88 between the series requiring actual assembly of objects and the printed picture tests (Stenquist, 1923).

At the invitation of the Psychology Committee of the National Research Council, chaired by Yerkes, a systematic six-year study of mechanical, manual, and spatial abilities was carried out at the University of Minnesota (Paterson, Elliott, Anderson, Toops, Heidbreder, 1930). Extensive test development was undertaken (several of the manual and spatial tests will be mentioned later). The Stenquist test involving assembly of mechanical objects was revised and extended to become the Minnesota Assembly Test, with considerably increased reliability. The Stenquist tests in the form of pictures were administered, with time limits for each part, thus increasing their reliabilities.

In the 1920's there was considerable activity in Germany in the development of tests for the selection of apprentices to be trained as machinists, tool makers, and workers in the metal trades. As a part of a battery of eighteen such tests, Rupp (1925) developed a Test of Technical Comprehension consisting of pairs of diagrams illustrating basic principles in mechanics and everyday physics. The subject was required to state which of the diagrams met a certain condition, thus indicating some knowledge of the principle involved. Some years later, the method

GEORGE K. BENNETT (BORN 1904)

Author of the Test of Mechanical Comprehension (1940) and co-author of the Differential Aptitude Tests (1947). President of the Psychological Corporation.

was applied very successfully in the development of the Bennett Test of Mechanical Comprehension (1940).

MOTOR TESTS

Early investigators of individual differences often used measures involving speed, accuracy, and strength of muscle action. Galton's battery included measures of strength of pull, swiftness of blow, and steadiness of hand. Cattell used dynamometer pressure and rate of movement. In *L'Année Psychologique* for 1898, Binet and Vaschide reported a series of eighteen studies (more than 300 pages of text) on motor tests, physiological measures, and anatomical data on school children. Whipple's 1910 Manual describes a number of manual measures, including tapping, aiming, tracing, and steadiness. While tests involving physical movement were soon found to have negligible relationships to school grades and measures of brightness, interest in them revived when psychologists began to investigate characteristics related to success in various industrial occupations. O'Connor (1928) developed a Finger Dexterity test and a Tweezer Dexterity test as practical selection devices. His Wiggly Block test was intended to involve not only manipulative ability but also three-dimensional perception.

A number of motor tests were developed at the University of Iowa under C. E. Seashore's direction, including the Koerth Rotary Pursuit (1922), used many years later as a psychomotor test to select pilots in World War II. R. H. Seashore (1930) extended the Iowa work by making a systematic study of motor tests; his finding was that they are reasonably reliable but measure quite independent abilities, with no evidence for a general factor.

The MacQuarrie Mechanical Ability Test (1927) was the first example of a printed group test used successfully to measure manipulative abilities. Of its seven parts, three—tracing, tapping, and dotting— seem to be motor measures, while others seem to measure perceptual and spatial abilities. Printed group tests to measure somewhat similar functions—tapping, accuracy of movement, aiming, and speed of movement—were included in the Minnesota study of mechanical abilities, mentioned earlier, which also included a number of apparatus tests of motor agility and accuracy.

SPATIAL ABILITIES

While tests measuring perception of spatial relations were rather slow to evolve, they soon became important in supplementing verbal measures of intelligence, and had specific validities for prediction of performance in certain occupations, such as engineering, where judgments of spatial relationships are important.

It will be recalled that form boards, involving both manipulation and spatial perception, have been important components of performance scales of intelligence. In World War I, the Army psychologists built the Army Beta, a non-language group test, as a companion to the Army Alpha. The Beta included a maze test (based on the earlier work of Porteus), a block counting test, and a geometrical construction test involving dividing a square into a set of component parts. Block counting and the construction test certainly are spatial measures and the maze test seems to have a spatial component. The Minnesota experiment involved the development of the Minnesota Paper Form Board, similar to the construction test of the Army Beta but more general in that there were many basic shapes to be divided into components, including circles, crosses, triangles, rectangles, and trapezoids in addition to squares. Later, Likert and Quasha (1934) published a multiple-choice revision, which made the test more objective and reduced scoring costs. With the development of batteries designed to yield scores on a number of more or less independent aptitudes, some test of spatial perception is a standard component.

THE MEASUREMENT OF INVENTIVENESS AND CREATIVITY

Both Binet (Binet and Henri, 1896) and Terman (1906) were involved in attempts to elicit creative behavior. Terman's discussion follows:

> It is clear that invention is largely dependent upon constructive imagination, the ability to abstract from present experience and picture new situations, their possibilities and their consequences. In both, images are united intentionally in order to form a new combination. It is imagination which invents. Reason is only a mode of control and justification. It determines values, accepts or rejects, but must get its raw material from creative imagination. Conjecture, which is only another name for the same thing, is at the basis of the most diverse scientific inventions. All sciences begin with hypotheses. All this means also the ability to profit by experience, to sift out the useful element from a manifold, to bring the past to bear upon the future, to join elements previously isolated. . . .
> We have above presented the view that at bottom all invention is one and the same thing. We are able, nevertheless, to mark out three sorts of inventive genius that differ somewhat from each other. They are, first, mechanical invention, involving a type of creative imagination that is exact, clear, objective, concrete, with little of the affective element. Second, artistic invention which is more emotional, subjective and romantic. Its imagery is somewhat less perceptual or concrete than that of mechanical invention, and it is more characteristic of dreamy and myth-making minds. Third, scientific and philosophical

invention, whose imaginative constructions are conceptual, schematic, abstract. . . .

It is probable that these three sorts of invention look more alike from without than from within. That is to say, while much alike if viewed objectively, they have each a peculiar affective tone that will make success in one a hindrance to success in another.

In line with this conceptualization, Terman developed a set of ten problems or puzzles which he hoped would tap inventiveness. In a group of seven bright and seven dull boys, he found some evidence that he was measuring creativity, probably of the mechanical variety, and that this trait was somewhat independent of intelligence.

Following Terman's pioneer investigation, numerous attempts have been made to analyze the nature of creative abilities and to develop devices to measure them. Despite the use of intriguing test material involving divergent thinking and fluency in recombining observations and ideas, creativity tests are largely experimental instruments because their utility in predicting actual inventiveness has not been satisfactorily demonstrated.

4

PERSONALITY
QUESTIONNAIRES AND
SPECIAL CLINICAL DEVICES

While Galton devised the questionnaire for use as a tool in psychological research, as in the investigation of imagery, it was R. S. Woodworth who during World War I applied the technique to the study of emotional stability. In so doing, he invented what was at first called a "personal data questionary," the lineal ancestor of all subsequent personality inventories, schedules, and questionnaires. An account in Woodworth's own words follows (Woodworth, 1951):

> The experience of other armies had shown that liability to "shell shock" or war neurosis was a handicap almost as serious as low intelligence. After considering other possible emotion tests, I concluded that the best immediate lead lay in the early symptoms of neurotic tendency which the neurologists and psychiatrists were finding in the case histories of neurotic subjects. Collecting hundreds of such symptoms from reported case histories, I threw them into the form of a questionnaire which could be applied to a group of subjects at a time, the single questions to be answered Yes or No. I tried this questionnaire on normal groups, and eliminated questions, or so-called symptoms, which were reported so frequently by the normal subjects that they could scarcely have any diagnostic value. The abridged questionnaire was tried on a thousand recruits in one of the camps, and on small groups of diagnosed abnormal subjects, and the results worked up again and submitted to a conference as-

ROBERT S. WOODWORTH (1869–1962)

Pioneer in the study of race differences (St. Louis World's Fair 1904); co-author of the Woodworth–Wells association tests (1911); author of the first personality inventory (1918).

sembled by the Surgeon General to advise him as to the military use of the questionnaire. The decision was to give the device a trial as part of the psychological examining procedure in one of the camps. Soon afterwards, the War came to a close, leaving the question unsettled as to whether or not the questionnaire would really assist in discovering the recruits who were specially susceptible to psychoneurosis. The idea was to use the quantitative score of unfavorable responses as a first indicator, to be followed up by individual examination at the psychiatrists' hands. At all stages of this work on the "Personal Data Sheet," I had valuable collaboration—that of Poffenberger in preparing the first draft, before he went into the Army, and that of Boring in securing the results from the Army samples. Hollingworth used the questionnaire on "shell shock" cases invalided home, with interesting results. Since the War, quite a number of psychologists have used the questionnaire or modified forms of it, and, though the results have never been striking, it still seems to have possibilities of usefulness.

Among the questions* which were found to differentiate somewhat between normals and abnormals were the following:

* The 116 items of the complete instrument are given in the Appendix.

Do you feel sad or low-spirited most of the time? Are you ever bothered with feeling that people are reading your thoughts?

Woodworth reported (1919) that of the 100 symptoms inquired about, the average college student reported about 10, the typical neurasthenic or hysteric at Camp Upton over 40, and returned "shell shock" cases at the Plattsburgh Reconstuction Hospital about 30.

LATER WORK WITH PRINTED PERSONALITY TESTS

In 1919 Pressey published the X-O Tests for Investigating the Emotions (Pressey and Pressey, 1919). Among the tasks: crossing out all words (in lists totaling 375) denoting situations or things considered unpleasant, blameworthy, or emotionally disturbing; identifying the word most unpleasant or blameworthy in each group of five; and finding the closest association (out of five) to a given stimulus word. Scoring was in terms of anxiety tendency and emotional idiosyncrasy. While Pressey's device was tried out in a number of investigations, his techniques have had only limited application in the measurement of personality characteristics. In contrast, Woodworth's method of asking numerous direct questions has been used in the development of numerous personality instruments. Several studies in the early 1920's using the Woodworth P-D Sheet (as it was called) or one of several modifications of it confirmed that the technique reflects the degree to which the individual is adequate in his adjustment to annoying situations.

In 1925 Laird published two "Personal Inventories" in which an item format was used; the respondent indicated the frequency or intensity of his feelings or reactions in regard to a question by marking along a scale with three or four terms defining degree. Assuming that traits which are characteristic of mental ill-health are exaggerations of traits of behavior present in all human beings, he arranged the items in one of the inventories in diagnostic groupings of clinical psychiatry: psychasthenoid, schizoid, neurasthenoid, and hysteroid. Questions in the second inventory were intended to measure introversion-extroversion, a concept used by Carl Jung with which psychologists of the day were beginning to be concerned.

Another attempt to use the questionnaire method to measure a personality trait, defined as a "characteristic form of behavior more generalized than the single reaction or simple habit," was the Ascendance-Submission test, conceived as early as 1921 but published seven years later (Allport, 1928). The method of the test was to present verbally certain life situations and to require the subject to select from

GORDON W. ALLPORT (1897–1967)

Author of the Ascendance–Submission Reaction Study (1928); co-author of A Study of Values, the first personality instrument to use ipsative scoring.

a few standardized choices that type of behavior which most nearly characterized his typical adjustment to each of the situations. The test was presented partly as a methodological contribution toward the objective study of personality.

An early questionnaire intended to be applied to surveys of school children whether or not they were evincing personality difficulties was the Adjustment Survey described by Symonds and Jackson (1930). The items were divided into seven sections, relating to adjustment to the curriculum, social life of the school, the administration, teachers, other pupils, home and family, and personal affairs.

At about the same time, the Thurstone Personality Schedule (Thurstone, 1930) was published, and it was designed to obtain an index of the neurotic tendencies of college freshmen. Some 600 items were collected from Woodworth's inventory and its revisions, from discussions of introversion-extroversion, and from the tests already published by Laird and the Allports. Most of the duplicate items were discarded, and the retained items were judged as to whether the neurotic would answer the question by encircling "yes," "no," or "?". Items were then evaluated by the method of internal consistency, essentially by correlating each item with the total score on the tentative key. Actually, an abbreviated procedure was used: counts of unfavorable responses were found for two groups of 50 subjects each, the 50 (out of 694) having the highest tentative total scores and the 50 having the lowest.

Using basically the same item sources that were used for the Thurstone schedule, but with some original items relating to self-sufficiency, the Bernreuter Personality Inventory was published in 1931. Its chief methodological innovation was that a single item could carry a weight in more than one of the four scales: neurotic tendency, self-sufficiency, introversion-extroversion, and dominance-submission. Bernreuter used three existing instruments, the Thurstone Personality Schedule, the Laird measure of introversion-extroversion, and the Allport Ascendance-Submission study, in addition to his self-sufficiency items to select extreme cases for his four sets of criterion groups. The final 125 items were weighted differentially by the technique which Strong had used in developing keys for his Vocational Interest Blank.

The Allport-Vernon Study of Values, published originally in 1931, was based on Eduard Spranger's (1928) sixfold classification of evaluative attitudes: the theoretical, the economic, the aesthetic, the social, the political, and the religious. In responding to items, subjects were required to make choices designed to reflect evaluative attitudes in specific situations. The six scores were intended to reveal the relative strengths of the six basic values within the individual. Since the six scores add to a constant, high scores in one or more areas are necessarily and automatically compensated for by one or more low scores on other value areas. This innovation has been called "ipsative" scoring, because comparisons are essentially within the self rather than between the individual and others.

THE MINNESOTA MULTIPHASIC PERSONALITY INVENTORY

Principles used in the early personality questionnaires have been applied extensively in instruments currently used in guidance counseling and in clinical psychology. In the development of the Minnesota Multiphasic Personality Inventory (Hathaway and McKinley, 1940), use was made of Woodworth's procedure of writing items that seemed to have clinical significance and establishing validity by contrasting the responses of normal and abnormal subjects.

STARKE R. HATHAWAY (BORN 1903)

Author (with J. C. McKinley) of the Minnesota Multiphasic
Personality Inventory (1940).

Hathaway and McKinley also used the model of the Strong Vocational Interest Blank in that a large item pool was created with the idea that only a relatively small subset would be included in any one key or scale. The entire pool, eventually 550 different items, selected from more than 1000 items and covering health conditions, habits, personal and social attitudes, and psychiatric symptoms, was administered both to normals and to individuals exhibiting a defined pathological condition, such as psychasthenia or schizophrenia. Items showing the greatest differentiation were selected for the scale, which was then cross-validated on new groups of cases. The items, written as declarative sentences, were in one form of the instrument printed on small cards to be sorted by the subject into three groups, "True," "False," and "Cannot say."

The MMPI item pool has been used to form diagnostic scales both by the original authors and by other investigators. An innovation was the development of several "validity" scales, designed to indicate such factors as the degree to which the subject is consistently selecting socially acceptable responses rather than telling the truth about himself.

The fifty items of the Taylor Manifest Anxiety Scale (Taylor, 1951), used in experimentation on the relationship of anxiety to performance, also were selected from the MMPI pool.

Few psychological devices have been subjected to greater scrutiny than the MMPI, with research reports numbering in the hundreds.

Hathaway has been an important contributor to this literature with the "Atlas" (Hathaway and Meehl, 1951), a landmark of empirical personality inventory research.

The principle of forcing choices, introduced in the Study of Values, has been modified and applied in various Q-sort tests, in the Kuder Preference Record—Personal, and in the Edwards Personal Preference Schedule. The latter instrument, like earlier introversion-extroversion measures and the Study of Values, has a theoretical orientation from an outside source—in this case Murray's system of needs.

Variants of Thurstone's method of selecting items by internal consistency have been widely applied in the development of personality questionnaires, with the techniques of sorting pools of items into more or less independent clusters constituting the chief recent innovation.

In the middle 1930's, J. P. Guilford (Guilford and Guilford, 1936) assembled large groups of items and separated them into subgroups by factor analytic techniques. The clusters were then named in accordance with the content of the items of which they were composed, and evidence of their validity was sought in the form of correlations with outside criteria.

Another application of factor analysis in test construction was made by R. B. Cattell (1945) in developing a series of personality tests, including the Sixteen Personality Factors Questionnaire. Cattell used the technique to determine the major groupings of trait names, prior to constructing items to measure relatively independent traits. The factor approach, which contrasts markedly with the direct empiricism of Woodworth and Hathaway, aims at constructing instruments which are useful in a wide variety of situations, including counseling of normal individuals.

THE DEVELOPMENT OF ASSOCIATION TESTS

Events which ultimately led to the development of association tests were reported by Galton (1879) as follows:

> No one can have a just idea, before he has carefully experimented upon himself, of the crowd of unheeded half-thoughts and faint imagery that flits through his brain, and of the influence they exert upon his conscious life. I will describe a few of the results of my own self-examination in respect to associated ideas. . . .

The plan I adopted was to suddenly display a printed word, to allow about a couple of ideas to successively present themselves, and then . . . to seize upon those ideas before they had faded, and to record them exactly as they were at the moment when they were surprised and grappled with. . . .

I procured a short vocabulary of words, and laid it open by my side. I then put a book upon it in such a way that it did not cover the word that was about to be displayed, though its edge hid it from my view when I sat a little backwards in my chair. By leaning forward the word came into sight. I also took many petty precautions . . . to prevent any other object besides the word catching my attention and distracting the thoughts. Before I began the experiment, I put myself into an easy position, with a pen in my right hand resting on a memorandum book, and with a watch that marked quarter seconds in my left hand, which was started by pressing on a stop, and continued going until the pressure was released. This was a little contrivance of my own appended to one of Benson's common chronographs. When I felt myself perfectly in repose, with my mind blank, but intent, I gently leant forward and read the word, simultaneously pressing the stop of the watch. Then I allowed about a couple of ideas to present themselves, and immediately afterwards released the stop and gave my utmost power of attention to appreciate with accuracy what had taken place, and this I recorded at once. Lastly, I wrote down at leisure the word that had been displayed, and the time shown by the chronograph to have been occupied by the experiment.

The number of words used in the experiments I am about to describe is seventy-five. . . .

I found the average interval that elapsed between displaying the word, and the formation of two successive ideas associated with it, to be a little less than two and a quarter seconds—say at the rate of fifty in a minute or three thousand in an hour. These ideas, it must be recollected, are by no means atomic elements of thought; on the contrary, they are frequently glimpses over whole provinces of mental experiences and into the openings of far vistas of associations, that we know to be familiar to us, though the mind does not at the moment consciously travel down any part of them. . . .

The seventy-five words gone through on four successive occasions made a total of 300 separate trials, and gave rise between them to 505 ideas in the space of 660 seconds. There were, however, so many cases of recurrence that the number of different ideas proved to be only 279. . . .

I divided such part of the 279 different ideas as admitted of it into groups, according to the period of my life when the association that linked the idea to the word was first formed, and found that almost exactly the half of those that recurred either twice, thrice, or four times, dated back to the period when I had not yet left college, at the age of twenty-two. Of those that did not recur in any of the trials the proportion that dated previously to the age of twenty-two to those of later date was a little smaller. . . .

The 279 different ideas fell into three groups. Those in fact and most numerous were characterised by a vague sense of acting a part. They might be compared to theatrical representations in which the actors were parts of myself, and of which I also was a spectator. . . .

The second group of ideas consists of mere sense of imagery, unaccompanied by any obscure feeling of muscular tension or action; such as mental landscapes, sounds, tastes, etc. . . .

The third and last group consisted of purely verbal associations, whether the mere names of persons or things, or bits of quotations in prose or verse. . . .

Experiments such as these allow an unexpected amount of illumination to enter into the deepest recesses of the character, which are opened and bared by them like the anatomy of an animal under the scalpel of a dissector in broad daylight. If we had records of the self-examination of many persons, and compared them, I think we should be much impressed by the differences between one mind and another, in the quality, wealth, and appropriateness of their associated ideas, and we should wonder that mutual misunderstandings were not more frequent even than they are. . . .

The more I have examined the workings of my own mind, whether in the walk along Pall Mall, or in the seventy-five words, or in any other of the numerous ways I have attempted but do not here describe, the less respect I feel for the part played by consciousness. I begin with others to doubt its use altogether as a helpful supervisor, and to think that my best brain work is wholly independent of it. The unconscious operations of the mind frequently far transcend the conscious ones in intellectual importance. Sudden inspirations and those flashings out of results which cost a great deal of conscious effort to ordinary people, but are the natural outcome of what is known as genius, are undoubted products of unconscious cerebration. Conscious actions are motivated, and motives can make themselves attended to, whether consciousness be present or not. Consciousness seems to do little more than attest the fact that the various organs of the brain do not work with perfect ease or cooperation. Its position appears to be that of a helpless spectator of but a minute fraction of a huge amount of automatic brain work. The unconscious operations of the mind may be likened to the innumerable waves that travel by night, unseen and in silence, over the broad expanse of an ocean. Consciousness may bear some analogy to the sheen and roar of the breakers, where a single line of the waves is lashed into foam on the shores that obstruct their course.

OTHER STUDIES OF ASSOCIATION

Galton was not, of course, the first scholar to be interested in association. More than 2,000 years earlier, Aristotle had proposed a classification scheme which was in vogue until modern times. The eighteenth-century mental philosophers, both in Great Britain and in France, used various principles of association as central concepts. The importance of Galton's work was that associations were experimentally evoked and quantitatively studied, thus bringing them into the field of science.

Wundt immediately recognized the importance of Galton's discoveries and began to study association with improved apparatus and methods. Cattell, while still in Wundt's laboratory, started work on association, and in 1889 he reported that he had been successful in making two types of quantitative determinations: time required for mental associations, and relative frequencies of associations of normal individuals to standard lists of words.

While Münsterberg was the pioneer in investigating association as a means of determining guilt, it has been in the study of the abnormal personality that the association method has had its greatest popularity. In addition to Kraepelin, whose work was described earlier, Aschaffenburg (1896), Jung (Jung and Riklin, 1904), an early associate of Freud, and Kent and Rosanoff (1910) all saw in the association technique a method of diagnosing mental illness. Jung's free association test consisted of 100 words to each of which the subject was to respond as quickly as possible with the first word coming to mind. The list, constructed after many years of experience, was intended to reveal complexes of various types by prolongation of reaction time and by response content. The Kent-Rosanoff tables of the reactions of 1,000 normal subjects to a list of 100 stimulus words were designed to provide a basis for comparing the reactions of normal and abnormal subjects.

While the free association test using words as stimuli had less than moderate success as a psychiatric diagnostic device, it was the forerunner of the "projective" instruments, which have seen considerable use in the description of personality and in clinical psychology.

CARL G. JUNG (1875–1961)

Psychiatrist who developed a word association test for the study
of personality (1904). A student of Jung's, Hermann Rorschach,
used ink blots as stimuli to elicit associations.

ORIGINS OF PROJECTIVE DEVICES:
THE RORSCHACH INKBLOT TEST

As early as 1896 Binet and Henri had pointed out in a study of
imagination the possibility that an inkblot could elicit differential response patterns (Binet and Henri, 1896). The major impetus to the
use of inkblots, however, came from the work of a young Swiss psychiatrist, Hermann Rorschach (1884–1922), who had studied at Zürich
and was familiar with Jung's verbal free association test. After many
trials Rorschach (1921) selected ten ink blots as chance or nonspecific
stimuli to be interpreted, one at a time, by the subject. Rorschach regarded the interpretation of chance forms having no intrinsic meaning
as a matter of perception rather than of imagination.

From the very first, responses to the Rorschach inkblots have been
evaluated not primarily in terms of the content of the associations
evoked, but rather in terms of classes or types of associations: the degree
to which they correspond to the actual forms; whether there is perception of movement; and whether there is reaction to the color in

HERMANN RORSCHACH (1884–1922)

A Swiss psychiatrist trained in part at Zurich, Rorschach devised
a series of inkblots to evoke associations used in personality
description.

certain of the inkblot plates. Rorschach, like scores of investigators
who have since used this method, attempted to relate various characteristics of responses, such as perception of the forms as wholes, attention to details, and responses to shading, to intellectual level, to
apperceptive type, and to psychiatric diagnosis, apparently with some
success.

In the United States the collaboration of a psychiatrist, David M.
Levy, and a psychologist, Samuel J. Beck, helped popularize the instrument, with Beck publishing a long series of contributions starting in
the early 1930's.

Increasing demand for the services of clinical psychologists in
child guidance centers, mental hygiene clinics, and neuropsychiatric
hospitals to work with psychiatrists in the diagnosis and treatment of
mental difficulties resulted in a felt need for appropriate diagnostic
instruments. By the 1930's the Binet scale and its descendants were
well-recognized devices for the estimation of intellectual level; at the
same time there was available an increasing array of measures of achievement, special aptitudes, and interests. In the description of personality,
however, questionnaires and rating forms had had very limited success.
Despite rather shaky evidence of relationship with personality criteria,
the Rorschach was welcomed by clinicians as a series of nonthreatening

stimuli which evoked significant material more or less spontaneously from subjects who otherwise might be reticent about describing themselves. It also became apparent that the nature of the responses was determined more by processes internal to the subject than by the characteristics of the inkblot stimuli.

Three tasks originally used by psychologists in the measurement of intelligence were modified into projective devices: the interpretation of pictures (used by Binet and appearing in various revisions of the Binet scale), sentence completion (devised by Ebbinghaus as an intelligence test), and drawing a human figure (scaled as a test by Goodenough).

THE THEMATIC APPERCEPTION TEST

Murray's Thematic Apperception Test (TAT), consisting of a series of highly ambiguous pictures (Morgan and Murray, 1935), has had, after the Rorschach, the widest acceptance by clinicians and investigators of personality. In the TAT a series of pictures, generally with human figures of recognizable age and sex, is shown to the subject

HENRY A. MURRAY (BORN 1893)

Author of *Explorations in Personality* (1938) and creator (originally with C. D. Morgan) of the Thematic Apperception Test.

one at a time, and he is instructed to make up a story to explain the situation as he understands it. Interpretation emphasizes the discovery of the felt needs and basic attitudes of the subject as revealed in the associative and imaginative content of the responses, and in his perceptions of the environmental forces surrounding him.

As with the Rorschach, the TAT is evaluated from a "protocol," a written record of the subject's responses, often taken from a tape recording. Interpretation yields an impressionistic description of the examinee, which often includes leads for further investigation.

SENTENCE COMPLETION AND OTHER PROJECTIVE METHODS

While Payne (1928) was the first to use sentence completion in the assessment of personality, its development has been the work of many individuals. The method involves presenting the subject with a form on which are printed a number of stems, such as "I often wish I _____" or "George frequently has difficulty _____." The subject is instructed to make each stem into a complete sentence, working as quickly as possible. How the sentences are completed gives clues to the examinee's motives and internal conflicts.

In 1939, Rohde received permission to revise the forty sentences of the Payne test. Subsequently there was considerable development of incomplete sentence forms in three World War II organizations, with some utilization of the Rohde items. In the O. S. S. Assessment Program (Murray *et al.*, 1948) experience with the method was promising and the form used went through a number of revisions. Not originally included in the testing program, sentence completion eventually became the only projective instrument in the battery of texts used with O.S.S. recruits.

Working in an AAF Convalescent Hospital, Benjamin Willerman and J. B. Rotter (Rotter, 1946) developed a forty-item incomplete sentence test which was modeled in part on a procedure developed by Cameron in a study of schizophrenics (Cameron, 1938). Cameron's work drew on Piaget for part of its theoretical formulation.

Willerman and Rotter found that when sentences were scored by comparing them one by one with sample responses already graded on a seven-point scale, satisfactory reliabilities were found and there was a good correlation with an independent evaluation of severity of disturbance.

Incomplete sentence tests were also used in Army installations with some success, and numerous forms were devised and revised. After World War II, various authors, including Rohde (1957) and Rotter and Rafferty (1950), brought out formal sentence completion tests.

Goodenough (1926), in her original work with children's drawings, noted that children with psychopathic tendencies sometimes made drawings that differed from those of normal children. She felt that children's drawings, properly understood, could contribute to knowledge of their interests and personality traits. A few years later Lembke (1930) noted that in crayon drawings, bold children outlined objects less distinctly and used dark, noncomplementary color combinations more frequently than shy children.

In the late 1940's, when clinical psychology was expanding rapidly, there was much interest in developing new projective techniques to be used along with what had become the standard instruments, the Rorschach and the TAT. Buck (1948) developed the H-T-P test, requiring the subject to draw a house, a tree, and a person. Machover (1949) published a monograph presenting the drawing of the human figure as a method of personality investigation. Her method involved the impressionistic interpretation of various signs by which drawings were to be placed in diagnostic categories.

In 1945, after a number of years of research, the Rosenzweig Picture Frustration Study was published as a semi-projective technique. In the form for adults there are twenty-four cartoon-like drawings, each representing a situation which is frustrating to one of the individuals depicted. The subject responds by writing the reply he thinks the thwarted individual might give. Considerable research has been carried out by Rosenzweig and others, and there has been some clinical use of the instrument. In both format and theory, it represents a definite departure from other projective approaches.

With the growing interest in the psychological description of personality characteristics, both for theoretical studies and in connection with therapy, a wide variety of ambiguous stimulus materials has been tried out, including cloud pictures, unstructured sounds, puppets, dolls and other toys, finger paintings, and comic strip characters. An excellent review of the origins and early theories of the projective methods is given by Sargent (1945).

TESTS OF ORGANICITY

An outgrowth of the use of psychological tests to measure behavioral characteristics has been their use for discovering abnormal conditions within the brain. Most psychological tests seek a sample of behavior that is indicative of other behavior; tests of "organicity" seek samples of behavior useful in detecting pathology of the nervous system.

Generations of neurologists have correlated externally observable behavior with organic conditions. While the X-ray, the electroencephalogram, and various physiological techniques have been major tools in the diagnosis of internal conditions, there has been a continuing need for more informative and simpler methods of differentiation. To numerous investigators the psychological test has been a promising lead. However, there is an important difference between the use of a psychological test to measure a trait and the use of a test to indicate brain damage. A trait is considered a continuous variable existing to a degree in everyone; a test in medical practice is often used to indicate whether an abnormal condition such as an infection or injury is or is not present.

In many areas of testing there have been relatively sudden developments, for which only a few people were mainly responsible. The history of testing for organicity has been different. Many individuals have carried out research projects to investigate the utility of existing tests for detecting brain damage and for differentiating between organic conditions and functional disorders. Knowledge has accumulated slowly and, in general, has been associated with application and adaptation of existing devices rather than the development of radically new instruments.

With several collaborators, Kurt Goldstein carried out a series of researches on the psychological concomitants of brain damage, beginning with a study in Germany of men wounded in World War I (Gelb and Goldstein, 1920). After concluding that individuals with critical injuries exhibit loss of ability to think abstractly and that their behavior comes to involve less generalization, he collaborated with Martin Scheerer in the publication of Tests of Abstract and Concrete Thinking (Goldstein and Scheerer, 1941). This set of five individual tests includes a modification of the Kohs Block Design test, a Color-Form Sorting test modified from one originally developed by Weigl (1941), a Color Sorting test, and an Object Sorting test based in part on the work of Gelb, and a Stick test involving the use of a kit of sticks. While some work has been done toward the quantification of these instruments, they are often interpreted in terms of signs that point to specific abnormalities, including brain injury and schizophrenia.

Attempts to diagnose organic brain pathology and to differentiate among psychiatric disorders have been made with the Bender-Gestalt, in which the subject is required to copy nine sample designs, originally used in studies of perception (Bender, 1938). Evidence as to its validity is not clear-cut, but its usefulness has been improved by a scoring system developed by Pascal and Suttell (1951).

The Memory-for-Designs test (Graham and Kendall, 1946) is an extension of a technique used by Binet in the measurement of intelligence. Fifteen cards, each with a simple design, are shown to the subject one at a time for five seconds. After each presentation the subject attempts to draw from memory what he has seen. A raw score, corrected for age and intelligence, provides reasonably good differentiation of functional disorders from those involving brain injury, especially when the test is supplemented with other information. Somewhat similar in purpose and method is a Visual Retention test published in 1945 by Benton.

Researches making psychological comparisons of persons with organic and nonorganic mental disorders have involved other forms of memory testing, such as digit span, differential scores on subtests of the Wechsler scales, picture completion, differences in speed of response, and signs on the Rorschach. Attempts have also been made by psychological methods to differentiate among various types of brain damage, with some success. A promising start in an area of testing that is of interest both to medicine and to psychology has been made.

ASSESSMENT

A notable program of global assessment of individuals began in 1943 in the organization that was the predecessor of the Central Intelligence Agency, that is, the wartime Office of Strategic Services.

Using methods first used in Germany but developed further in a British program for selecting Army officers, some sixty American psychologists set up stations, in the United States and abroad, where candidates for a wide variety of sensitive assignments, including operations behind enemy lines, were evaluated by an armamentarium of techniques. In both planning and execution, the project was the work of group thinking. It involved a number of psychologists who already had attained distinction, including Henry A. Murray, principal author of the TAT, and others who became well known later.

What was new in the assessment program was its broad perspective. Instead of attempting to measure rather limited aspects of behavior as had been the case with most psychometric and clinical devices up to that time, a program was designed to describe the way the individual was able to act in a wide variety of situations, including those involving extreme stress.

In one of the stations near Washington, recruits in fatigue uniforms assumed a false identity and developed a cover story, which the staff members during the three-day stay endeavored to break. The procedures described in a comprehensive report (OSS Assessment Staff, 1948) were varied: casual conversations, searching interviews, the sentence completion test, questionnaires about health and working conditions and personal history, conventional aptitude tests such as map memory and mechanical comprehension, and a number of situational tests.

Tests for the evaluation of intelligence that involve the examiner as an integral part of the situation go back to Binet. The tests devised by the OSS psychologists, however, were aimed at eliciting consistent behavior patterns indicative of ability to cope with a variety of highly demanding situations. In the Brook situation (in which fancy and fact were commingled), a group of four to seven recruits were required to develop and execute a plan to convey heavy objects across a stream under prescribed conditions and with limited materials. Its aim was to elicit initiative, effective intelligence, and leadership. In the Construction problem, a single candidate was instructed to direct two "assistants" in building a frame structure out of simple wooden materials. The assistants acted roles of following orders literally but with as many obstructions and annoyances as possible. No candidate ever succeeded in this examination, which was used to assess emotional stability, frustration tolerance, and social relations. In the Resourcefulness test, the candidate was given a few minutes to construct a cover story to explain why he happened to be in a government building without identification and examining secret files at night. Interrogators behind a spotlight grilled a candidate for ten minutes in an attempt to break his story.

In later validity studies overseas performances of 1187 men were rated and described by superior officers and associates. Considering the extreme heterogeneity of the criteria, reasonably satisfactory validities were obtained. With few exceptions validity coefficients were positive and in some samples ranged up to figures such as .35 and .53.

Some ten years later, in a review of work on assessment (Cronbach, 1956), the attempt to use the global method in civilian projects was reported to have been unsuccessful. Nevertheless the situational test involving more complex behavior than is possible with the usual psychometric device remains a potentially useful tool.

5

THE MODERN
PERIOD IN PSYCHOMETRICS

The pioneering stage in psychometrics may be considered to have ended in the 1930's. Since then there has been increasing professionalism both in the development of tests and in their uses. No longer is test development a part-time activity of experimental psychologists using laboratory equipment for the study of individual differences, as was the case with Cattell, Binet, and Seashore. Many of the current leaders in testing have taken specialized doctoral degrees and work full time in the development and application of tests. The result has been the growth of a more or less autonomous body of knowledge which is called test theory.

In many instances it is difficult to ascribe a given development to a single individual. Intercommunication among an increasing number of professionals in test development and test theory through frequent formal meetings and a growing number of journals carrying technical articles has resulted in such a mass of activity that it often must be described in terms of movements rather than individual actions. Of course, leaders can be identified from time to time, but the sources of ideas are often obscure.

THE DEVELOPMENT OF TEST THEORY

The first book on psychological statistics was written by Thorndike, who had learned quantitative methods from Franz Boas, the anthropologist, as well as from Cattell. Thorndike's *An Introduction to the Theory of Mental and Social Measurements* appeared in 1904, the year of Spearman's paper on attenuation and the year before Binet's first intelligence scale. The 1921 volume on psychological examining in the U. S. Army (Yerkes, 1921) contained full explanations of the test development and statistical methods employed in the mass program in World War I. Shortly thereafter, two men who had studied with Thorndike published books which included new statistical developments of

PAUL HORST (BORN 1903)

Founder (with L. L. Thurstone and others) of *Psychometrika* and an early managing editor.

interest in psychological testing: McCall's *How to Measure in Education* (1922) and Kelley's *Statistical Method* (1923). In 1935, Horst and Thurstone and their associates founded *Psychometrika*, a journal which is devoted to the development of psychology as a quantitative, rational science and which took over from older journals the task of publishing articles of special interest in test theory. *Educational and Psychological Measurement* began to appear in 1941, the *British Journal of Statistical Psychology* in 1947. The latest journal in quantitative psychology is *Multivariate Behavioral Research*, which began publication in 1966.

Test theory as developed up to 1931 was summarized by Thurstone in *The Reliability and Validity of Tests*. Five years later came a more comprehensive book, *Psychometric Methods*, by J. P. Guilford (1936a). In these two publications methods of determining validity by correlation with a criterion were described and methods of determining reliability, basically dating back to Spearman, were presented. The three classical

J. P. GUILFORD (BORN 1897)

Author of *Psychometric Methods* (1936), Guilford has conducted extensive research on the nature of intellect and of creativity.

means of determining reliability were: test-retest (repeating the instrument on two occasions with the same group of subjects and correlating the results); correlation of alternative forms; and the split-half method (dividing the test into two portions considered to be equivalent, correlating the two scores for a group of subjects, and estimating the reliability of the whole by the Spearman-Brown "prophecy formula").

A major break-through in test theory came with publication in *Psychometrika* of "The theory of estimation of test reliability" (Kuder and Richardson, 1937). In this article the important formula was the twentieth presented and is generally known as "K-R 20." It was later rederived, using less restrictive assumptions. K-R 20 has developed into a general method of estimating reliability by correlating an existing test with its theoretical equivalent, which is considered to have the same standard deviation as the existing test, and to have items with relationships with existing items that are similar to their own interrelationships. This approach to reliability has been important in much subsequent development, including the concept of a test measuring an identifiable psychological characteristic.

One of the new concepts coming into test theory was that of homogeneity (Loevinger, 1947), in which a test is thought of as a collection of items measuring the same general function. Various routines for selecting items exhibiting homogeneity have been used in the construction of new tests.

A center of activity in the development of test theory has been the College Entrance Examination Board, where Carl Brigham was a pioneer in scientific item analysis methods. In addition to arranging items in

CARL C. BRIGHAM (1890–1943)

A pioneer in the systematic use of item analysis, Brigham established much of the strategy used in test development by such organizations as the College Entrance Examination Board and the Educational Testing Service.

approximate order of difficulty, as had been done earlier, Brigham emphasized both correlating items against external criteria and correlating them against total score, thus insuring greater internal consistency.

Another topic to which considerable attention has been given is the analysis of the kinds of validity that a psychological test may have. In 1954 a committee of the American Psychological Association accepted four types of validity, two of them involving correlation with an external criterion and two of them based on considerations which are partially internal to the instrument. In criterion-related validity, a distinction is made between the situation in which criterion data are available during test development (concurrent validity) and the situation in which criterion data become available at a later time (predictive validity). Recently this distinction has been minimized. In content validity, which is largely applicable to achievement tests, the items cover a defined subject matter area. In construct validity, the items are considered as measuring a definable psychological characteristic. Internal consistency of the items is one aspect of construct validity, but more pertinent is whether or not behavior on the test makes possible predictions of other types of behavior.

The concern with better descriptions of test validity is one further bit of evidence of the increasing sophistication of test developers in the 1950's. In an important paper (Campbell and Fiske, 1959), issues were raised on the scientific nature of psychological measurement. It was pointed out that for a psychological trait to be considered identified, its measurements by two different methods should correlate higher than measures of supposedly different characteristics using the same modes of observation.

The issue of response sets (Cronbach, 1946) was essentially a description of bias in personality inventories and interests tests, in which responses may reflect what the respondent feels are desirable answers.

In addition to a number of textbooks on psychological testing and test theory, two important summaries were published, by Gulliksen (1950) and Lord and Novick (1968). The Lord and Novick book is notable for extending principles of statistical inference to test theory. It emphasized the introduction of relevant mathematical and statistical models in psychological testing.

Relationships of decision theory to psychometrics were presented in a monograph, *Psychological Tests and Personnel Decisions* (Cronbach and Gleser, 1957), which delineated the conceptual framework of the situations in which tests have been found useful.

A majority of the statistical techniques useful in test development date back to the English statisticians. However, Richardson and Stalnaker (1933) developed the formula for the point biserial correlation, an algebraic variant of Pearson's product-moment r which is useful in correlating test items with continuous variables, such as total test score or an outside criterion.

A new technique which has had great impact on psychological testing is multiple factor analysis (Thurstone, 1931b, 1935). Experimental batteries and item pools have been factored to identify underlying variables. The development of all the multifactor batteries have their roots in Thurstone's methodology. Multiple factor analysis has been elaborated through the work of numerous investigators, so that Thurstone's numerical methods are largely of historical interest. His basic concept, that a variable can be broken into a number of additive components representing underlying characteristics, remains. These factors may be either uncorrelated or correlated.

An interesting improvement in test development procedure is the use of item rationales (Flanagan, 1951). The method begins with a list of behaviors to be sampled or predicted. Specifications are written for items that aim at measuring each of the behaviors on the list. The chief

JOHN C. FLANAGAN (BORN 1906)

Architect of the World War II Army Air Forces Aviation Psychology Program (which included test validation on an unprecedented scale), Flanagan originated the critical incident technique and Project Talent.

advantage is a systematic approach to test development, both in terms of the area to be covered and in terms of the specific function of each item in attaining the overall objective of the instrument.

TEST PUBLISHING

Many of the early printed tests were distributed by their authors or by university bookstores. Typically, early publishers merely printed and distributed the work of a test author.

A pioneer in test publishing was the World Book Company (which later merged to form Harcourt, Brace and World), with a long list of educational and psychological tests, including the Otis Group Intelligence Scale (1918). In 1921 Cattell, with the help of Thorndike and Woodworth, founded the Psychological Corporation to provide a variety of psychological services, with test publishing eventually becoming one of its most important functions. The Cooperative Test Service (now a part of the Educational Testing Service) was established in 1930, with Ben D. Wood as its director, to develop and publish high school and college tests, chiefly in the achievement area. These organizations were among the first to engage directly in systematic test development. In the two decades following World War I, the number of test publishers became very large—a 1936 directory had 96 entries.

In recent years test publishing has continued to develop in number of tests available, in volume of business, and in services offered to test users. In many cases, scoring services, tabulation of results, and even individual interpretations have been made available. Several test publishing organizations have been purchased by businesses interested in book publishing and education. Thus, Science Research Associates became a subsidiary of International Business Machines Corporation, the California Test Bureau was purchased by McGraw-Hill and the Psychological Corporation was bought by Harcourt, Brace and World.

One of the persistent problems with psychological tests has been how to insure their proper use. To this end, test publishers place restrictions upon who is permitted to buy tests. Some tests which are relatively easy to administer and interpret are sold to any reputable business organization, whereas others are restricted to organizations having access to acceptable professional assistance or to individuals with appropriate training and experience.

TEST SCORING MACHINES AND COMPUTERS

An important mechanical development in 1934 was the invention of the first test scoring machine,* the need for which had been envisaged several years earlier by Ben D. Wood. While Wood, several members of his staff of Columbia University, and engineers from the International Business Machines Corporation were experimenting with various approaches to the problem, Reynold B. Johnson, a high school science teacher, developed a novel method by which the number of

* An account is given by Downey (1965).

AN EARLY MODEL OF THE IBM TEST SCORING MACHINE (1935). This machine was developed by Reynold B. Johnson to read pencil marks on separate answer sheets.

electrically conductive graphite pencil marks in predetermined positions on a sheet of paper could be reliably read from an ammeter. Immediately the device had several consequences for testing:

1) It greatly lessened costs by reducing the labor involved in scoring tests.
2) It reduced costs by the introduction of a separate sheet for recording answers, making test booklets reusable.
3) It stimulated the growth of large testing programs by making mass processing of test results feasible.
4) It accelerated the trend toward more or less complete reliance on objective items, especially the multiple-choice item.

For nearly 20 years the original IBM test scoring machine was virtually unchallenged. When better machines finally were developed, they tended to be digital in principal rather than analog, they were adapted to handle test papers automatically, and they provided for automatic recording of results, ultimately within a computer system. The first of the electronic systems was developed by E. F. Lindquist at the University of Iowa. The systems developed later used somewhat similar principles, including optical pick-up of responses. Often the test responses are first read into a computer system and in subsequent stages the scores are computed and reported. For large-scale testing programs, scoring and reporting have become largely automatic.

A parallel development involved methods of scoring tests with numerous subscores and differential weighting of items, especially the Strong Vocational Interest Blank. The first break-through involved an application of the card-controlled electric accounting machine, which reduced costs to perhaps a tenth of earlier hand scoring procedures. Later methods, including the use of machines especially developed for this type of scoring, have been even more efficient.

Psychologists working with tests also found mechanical devices for computation exceedingly helpful in the increasing number of large programs. Card-sorting machines were used in 1919 in analyzing the results obtained with the Army Alpha and related tests. In computing the intercorrelations of variables in a 1928–32 study of achievement in Pennsylvania high schools and colleges, the staff of the Columbia Statistics Bureau developed a new procedure using punched card electric accounting machines, and the use of such machines soon became standard in all large testing programs. When large electronic computers began to be available in the 1940's, psychologists and educators working with quantitative data were among the first to utilize them.

In recent years computations of intercorrelations of test results, factor analyses of tables of intercorrelations, development of multiple regression equations, and various types of item analyses have been done routinely through the use of high-speed electronic computers. Internal consistency reliability, and some kinds of item analysis are often computed as by-products of test scoring within a computer system. As the electronic computers have developed large capacity for the storage of information and for large-scale arithmetic computation, costs of the analysis of test data have been reduced. This means that in large-scale testing programs knowledge of what the tests are doing and development of information for revising them is readily available.

This does not indicate that all psychological testing is on a high level of sophistication. Many school systems and industrial organizations administer tests without subsequent research on their utility. As testing has increased in small organizations, desirable follow-up studies have all too often been neglected.

MILITARY TESTING IN WORLD WAR II

All three United States military organizations: the Navy, the Army, and the Army Air Forces (which became the U. S. Air Force after the war) had extensive psychological testing programs during World War II. In 1939, when it seemed that war was about to break out in Europe, a Personnel Testing Section was established in the Office of the Adjutant General of the Army. The main emphasis was on the development of instruments to facilitate the classification of recruits and to aid in making job assignments. The Army General Classification Test (AGCT) was devised as a modernized version of the intelligence test which the Army had used in World War I, the Army Alpha. Walter V. Bingham, a member of the committee that designed the 1917 examination, was the chairman of an advisory committee established in 1940. The AGCT at first utilized only an overall score, but eventually it had four part scores as well: reading and vocabulary, arithmetic computation, arithmetic reasoning, and spatial relations. By the end of the war it had been administered in its various forms to over 9,000,000 men. Supplemental tests also were developed, including measures of mechanical and clerical aptitude, aptitude for code learning, and oral trade tests. All of these developments were along familiar lines.

The Navy also developed a general classification test and a number of devices to measure specific aptitudes. Considerable effort was expended in the refinement of personality measures. The Cornell Selectee Index, essentially a personality questionnaire, proved to have considerable validity in detecting recruits with potential emotional difficulties. This was in the tradition inaugurated by Woodworth three decades earlier.

In the Army Air Forces a program initiated by Colonel John C. Flanagan, who had been assistant director of the Cooperative Test Service under Ben D. Wood, exhibited considerable originality. Its first mission was to develop aptitude tests for the selection of trainees for three aircrew specialties: pilot, bombardier, and navigator (Flanagan, 1948). Job analyses of these specialties were coordinated with an energetic program of test development and validation. A system was established for relating test information and personal data to success in training and in later operations for all aircrew specialties. This was the most systematic program of test validation established up to that time, and follow-up studies were conducted on more than 185,000 men.

Another innovation was large-scale testing with a group of psychomotor tests which were administered as a part of the aircrew battery. The tests varied from time to time, but one of the most useful was the Complex Coordination test, involving lights controlled by a stick and rudder bar. This was a descendant of a job sample test developed in 1926 by L. J. O'Rourke of the U. S. Civil Service Commission and modified by Colonel Neely C. Mashburn eight years later, again in the AAF program. The Rotary Pursuit test was a descendant of an apparatus built by Wilhelmine Koerth in 1922. It involved a rotating target with which the examinee attempted to maintain contact with a stylus. A Two-Hand Coordination test was based on a somewhat similar device which had been found valid for the prediction of success of Naval cadets in flying training (McFarland and Channell, 1944). Another test, Rudder Control, modeled after an anti-groundloop trainer for students in elementary flying training, was another useful test of the job-sample type. The Discrimination Reaction Time test, involving reactions to the spatial relationships of different color lights, resembled earlier reaction time tests.

The validity of the pilot stanine, a composite score based on both printed and apparatus tests, with graduation-elimination from the first phase of pilot training as the criterion, was .50. The validity of the printed tests against the same criterion was approximately .40, and the validity of the psychomotor battery was also .40. The psychomotor tests thus added appreciably to the validity of the printed tests.

WORLD WAR II AVIATION CADETS BEING EXAMINED WITH THE COMPLEX COORDINATION TEST. Original elements of this test were developed by O'Rourke in 1926. Subsequently it was improved at the AAF School of Aviation Medicine by N. C. Mashburn.

An important study was conducted on 1143 aviation cadets who were sent into training with no selection either on the basis of psychological tests or psychiatric interview. All were volunteers for pilot training, however, and they met the usual physical standards. Of this group who were allowed to enter pilot training without psychological and psychiatric screening, only 23 per cent became rated pilots. As expected, the computed validity of the selection battery for this group was considerably increased, since the cadets represented a greater range of talent than those normally sent into training. Typical validities for the pilot aptitude score for cadets surviving preliminary screening had been of the order of .50. In the experimental group, the validity was .66. The study conclusively demonstrated the usefulness of psychological tests for screening purposes. Its clear-cut results were partially responsible for the prominent functions psychological tests were assigned in personnel operations when the United States Air Force was formed in 1948. An Airmen's Battery for classification of enlisted men was assembled at the Personnel Research Laboratory at Lackland Air Force Base. It was designed to measure aptitudes and interests important in all the usual Air Force specialties. The design of this battery called for a number of independent measures, to be weighted differentially, on the base of multiple regression, for the different training programs available to those enlisting in the Air Force.

One wartime innovation was an extensive program of development of motion picture testing under the direction of J. J. Gibson (1947). This was an exploration of a medium hitherto unexploited for psychological measurement. Several tests were developed which had validity for aircrew selection, but the variance was not sufficiently unique to warrant inclusion of the tests in the classification battery. On the other hand, a motion picture proficiency test for measuring skill in navigation (Carter, 1947) seemed to be of considerable potential importance.

Another development in military testing was the use of the Armed Forces Classification Test beginning in 1950. This was the first screening test used by all services to determine mental fitness, and it was designed to insure appropriate allocation of talent to all branches.

DIFFERENTIAL BATTERIES

For approximately three decades, beginning in the early part of the century, Spearman's two-factor theory of intelligence was accepted by many psychologists. As stated earlier, Spearman believed that a single general factor, which he called g, accounted for the intercorrelations among intellectual tests. It was called the two-factor theory because each test was conceived as a combination of g and an additional factor specific to it. This theory, although widely accepted, was not believed literally. Spearman himself admitted the existence of group factors, appearing in several tests but not as general as g. Thorndike had encouraged Stenquist to develop a test of mechanical intelligence, and Moss (Moss *et al.*, 1927) had attempted to develop a test of social intelligence.

In 1929 Schneck, using Spearman's tetrad analysis, demonstrated that two important types of material which had been widely used in intelligence tests, verbal items and numerical items, constitute two relatively independent factors. He demonstrated that verbal tests had high intercorrelations among themselves, as did numerical tests, but between the two types the correlations were only moderate. A few years later, applying his newly developed technique of multiple factor analysis, Thurstone demonstrated the existence of a number of relatively independent components* of what had been lumped together as intellectual ability.

With the new orientation toward factors, it was a natural development to make separate tests to measure them, all in the framework of a comprehensive battery. The precedent for a series of separate scores had already been set in interest and personality testing and in the measurement of specific aptitudes and skills. Thurstone developed the Chicago Tests of Primary Mental Abilities to measure the factors which had turned up in his factor analysis. Somewhat later in the Army Air Forces program, an aptitude battery of some twenty tests was weighted differentially for the several aircrew specialties. The United States Employment Service reported its new general aptitude test battery, called the GATB, shortly after World War II (Dvorak, 1947). The basic idea was soon translated into batteries available through commercial publishers, such as the Differential Aptitude tests, the Guilford-Zimmerman Aptitude Survey, and the Flanagan Aptitude Classification tests.

The multiple score battery resulted in flexibility both in counseling and in selection programs. In counseling the profile of aptitudes has given information as to relative strengths and weaknesses. In selection and classification programs, a general battery can be applied as a whole or in parts. The fact that norms on all subtests are directly comparable adds to their meaningfulness.

DEVELOPMENT OF TESTING PROGRAMS

An early systematic testing program was that of the College Entrance Examination Board, founded in 1900. Prior to that time many of the colleges and universities had been using admission examinations, but on an individual basis and without a systematic plan. The foundation of the College Entrance Examination Board provided common

---

* Among these were verbal ability and numerical ability discovered earlier by Schneck.

examinations which could be used by all of the participating members.

For many years only essay examinations were used. After the development of the multiple-choice item during World War I and experimentation with objective testing at Columbia College, objective tests were introduced into the program of the Board, including a scholastic aptitude test, a general measure of ability to do college work.

Beginning in the 1930's and continuing after World War II, a number of specialized testing programs came into existence. One of the first was the National Teachers Examination, sponsored by the American Council on Education under a foundation grant and executed by the Cooperative Testing Service. The examination includes tests of verbal ability and reasoning, professional knowledge, and various subject areas, and it has been used by numerous school systems in the selection of teachers. Other nationwide programs, with tests given to large groups of candidates at predetermined times and places involve admission to medical schools, law schools, schools of business, and other professional types of training.

The common characteristic of these testing programs is a central organization which assembles the tests and arranges for their administration at testing centers, generally at schools and colleges. The tests are not published and usually are carefully controlled. Often they include sections which are not scored but which are made up of items for analysis and possible inclusion in later forms.

In 1947 the Educational Testing Service was founded by three major educational groups active in testing: the American Council on Education, the Carnegie Foundation for the Advancement of Teaching, and the College Entrance Examination Board. The groups combined their testing functions to provide a unified, efficient organization to meet the measurement needs of American education. The chief center is in Princeton, New Jersey. In addition to the development of tests for various purposes and the administration of testing programs, ETS has become a major center of psychometric research.

THE WECHSLER SCALES

Improvements in the measurement of intelligence were made by David Wechsler, beginning with the Wechsler-Bellevue Intelligence Scale in 1939, which was composed of subscales so that a given type of task or item was administered only once. The I.Q. became a standard score with a mean of 100 at each age level and a standard deviation such that 50 per cent of the I.Q.s were between 90 and 110. The instrument

DAVID WECHSLER (BORN 1896)

Author of the Wechsler–Bellevue Intelligence Scale (1939) and
its successors: The Wechsler Adult Intelligence Scale, the
Wechsler Intelligence Scale for Children, and the Wechsler
Pre-School and Primary Scale of Intelligence.

yielded a verbal I.Q., a performance I.Q., and a total I.Q., thus reducing
the need for the earlier performance scales. A notable change in content made this test more suitable for adults than earlier scales had been.
The original 1939 scale has now been replaced by the Wechsler Adult
Intelligence Scale, the Wechsler Intelligence Scale for Children, and
the Wechsler Preschool and Primary Scale of Intelligence, which have
characteristics similar to the original Wechsler scale.

TEST STANDARDS

A bibliography of mental tests was published by Hildreth in 1933.
This was followed two years later by Buros' *Educational, Psychological,
and Personality Tests of 1933 and 1934*, which was the forerunner of a
comprehensive and indispensable series of Mental Measurements Yearbooks (Buros, 1938 and later) containing critical reviews of the most
important tests. These yearbooks have been very influential in setting
standards for the development and publication of devices for psychological measurement.

OSCAR K. BUROS (BORN 1905)

Originator and editor of the *Mental Measurements Yearbooks,* which have contributed notably to the maturity of psychological testing.

The healthy tendency of psychologists concerned with testing to adopt a critical attitude toward both the tests themselves and their applications resulted in 1954 in an important document, "Technical Recommendations for Psychological Tests and Diagnostic Techniques," published by the American Psychological Association. It represented the thinking of three organizations: the American Psychological Association, the American Educational Research Association, and the National Council on Measurement in Education. It set up standards for test manuals, particularly the types of information which should be developed before a test is made available for use, including information about reliability, validity, administration and scoring, and standardization. Twelve years later, a revised and expanded version was published as *Standards for Educational and Psychological Tests and Manuals* (APA, 1966). The existence of these standards, which were generally accepted by both test developers and test users, has undoubtedly increased the quality of psychological testing, at least in the English-speaking world.

PROFESSIONAL ORGANIZATIONS

After psychological testing began to play a role in education, government, and industry, test development and administration became professional specialties. Various organizations with primary and secondary interests in the field came into being. The Psychometric Society was organized in 1935 and has sponsored regular meetings for the presentation of new methodological developments and substantive research. When the American Psychological Association was reorganized in 1945, Division 5, the Division of Evaluation and Measurement, became one of its major components. Its annual programs have emphasized test theory and applications. Scientific papers involving psychological testing often appear in the programs of other divisions, such as the Divisions of Clinical Psychology, Industrial Psychology, and Educational Psychology. Other professional organizations with interests in psychological testing include the American Personnel and Guidance Association, the National Council on Measurement in Education, and other professional organizations made up of educators, counselors, and professionals in the field of personnel.

Beginning rather informally in 1936 under a different name, there has come into being an annual Invitational Conference on Testing Problems sponsored by the Educational Testing Service. *Testing Problems in Perspective* (Anastasi, 1966) presented a selection of papers from these conferences under three main headings: test development and use, psychometric theory and method, and special problems in the assessment of individual differences.

FURTHER DEVELOPMENTS OF MEASUREMENT TECHNIQUES

As mentioned earlier, Thorndike in World War I found a relationship between athletic skills as reported by candidates and later success in learning to fly. Goldsmith (1922) and Russell and Cope (1925) both reported that personal history data could be used in selecting life insurance salesmen. Among the items that Goldsmith found differentiating were: educational status (high school graduation optimal), age (the thirties being the best), membership in clubs, prior investment in life insurance, being married, and having confidence in one's own ability to sell.

Prior to World War II, a civilian investigation found that the biographical facts reported by candidates added appreciably to the value of the aptitude tests used for predicting flying success. This method was used later both by the Navy and the Army Air Forces. More recently, biographical data have been used to predict success in college, length of stay in a neuropsychiatric hospital, and research competence. The technique of developing a predictive instrument from biographical items reported by the subject seems to be well established.

A test which simulates aspects of adminstration was developed a decade after the OSS pioneering in situational testing (Frederiksen, Saunders, and Wand, 1957). The "in-basket technique" has been applied in selecting and training administrators in the military establishment, in education, and in business. It is administered in the form of memoranda, letters, notes on phone calls which have theoretically collected in the in-basket of an administrative officer. Background information about the institution is supplied to the examinee, and he is instructed to deal with the material in front of him. He is required to write memoranda and letters and to prepare agenda for meetings just as though he was actually on the job. The technique is amenable to the development of reasonably objective scoring procedures.

PROJECT TALENT

A long-range investigation of the usefulness of psychological testing was proposed by John Flanagan in 1957, and testing of some 140,000 students in 1353 secondary schools in all parts of the country was accomplished in March, 1960. The aim of Project Talent is to explore psychological methods for the identification and utilization of human abilities. Some twenty-three aptitude and achievement tests, covering most of the abilities discovered through factor analysis and comprehensive inventories of activities, interests, and preferences, were administered. Numerous analyses have already been made of the results. The plan is to follow up on the experiences of the group, looking for relationships between the early measurements and later events (Flanagan, 1962).

The project has been designed to collect systematic information in several areas: an estimate of the size of the manpower pool qualified for advanced professional training, better knowledge of the intercorrelation patterns of socioeconomic factors, aptitudes and interests, factors which limit achievement, factors affecting choice of vocation, indicators of creativity, effectiveness of various types of educational experience in developing talents, and methods for assisting individuals to realize their highest potential. This comprehensive psychological study is expected to continue well into the twenty-first century.

CRITICISMS OF TESTING

The very success of psychological testing has brought with it considerable criticism. One important objection relates to achievement tests and comes from educators who feel that responses to short-answer items do not reveal whether or not students have met some of the important objectives of education, such as coherent self-expression. Most psychometricians would be quick to point out numerous well-established advantages of objective testing, including the range of skills and knowledge that can be readily and systematically sampled, but they also would admit that reliance upon a single type of item, such as multiple-choice items, could have the unfortunate effect of overemphasizing a particular mode of response.

Another objection raised particularly in relation to personality questionnaires used for selection purposes, is the issue of invasion of privacy. In 1965 (Amrine) two different congressional committees investigated the issue, with a number of psychologists, lawyers, and public officials appearing as witnesses. Conflicting points of view were clearly presented, and there resulted better understanding of the issues both inside and outside the government. As clinical instruments, personality inventories continue to have wide acceptance, but there is now increased caution in their use for selection purposes.

A new issue in psychological testing arose in 1963, when a rejected applicant filed a charge of unfair employment practice before the Illinois Fair Employment Practice Commission, stating that he was rejected for employment because of race. At issue was the use of an aptitude test which the applicant was alleged to have failed and which he claimed was discriminatory.

The question of the fairness of psychological tests to individuals of different backgrounds is one that has evoked both discussion and action. In 1968 the U. S. Department of Labor issued instructions to government contractors requiring that when tests are used to determine qualifications for hire, transfer, or promotion in nonprofessional, technical, and managerial occupations definite empirical data demonstrating test validity be developed. It directed that as far as possible evidence of criterion-related validity be obtained and that results be examined for implication of possible discrimination against members of minority groups. While many industrial organizations had already been conducting validity studies more or less routinely, this official step put psychological testing procedures in the framework of a government regulation.

PSYCHOMETRICS AS TECHNOLOGY

Year by year, with the accretion of improved tests and better techniques, psychometrics has been gradually transformed from an art to an established technology. Any one of a number of dates might be taken as the date of the completion of the major part of this transformation: 1931, the year of the introduction of multiple factor analysis; 1941, the year psychometrics was mobilized for World War II; or 1954, the date of the publication of "Technical Recommendations for Psychological Tests and Diagnostic Techniques." Certainly by the middle 1950's the technique of developing a new test was well known; administration, scoring, and interpretation had been formalized; textbooks and courses had multiplied; statistical methods were well understood; and there was a large number of professionally trained psychologists and educators who could undertake almost any psychometric assignment.

Testing by psychologists began in the nineteenth century as the work of relatively isolated individuals. As it became useful, with the development of the Binet scale, the Army Alpha, and objective educational testing, more and more individuals became involved. Much of the energy of recent decades has gone into modest improvements in existing measures and relatively slight modifications in their applications. As in other areas of modern civilization, we can expect changes from time to time, but the innovations are likely to be the products of group thinking and the work of numerous well-trained professionals, who will remain indebted to the psychometric pioneers of the past.

BIBLIOGRAPHY

Abelson, A. R., The measurement of ability of backward children, *British Journal of Psychology*, 1911, *4*, 268-314.

Allport, F. H., and G. W. Allport, Personality traits: their classification and measurement, *Journal of Abnormal Psychology*, 1921, *16*, 6-40.

Allport, G. W., A test for ascendance-submission, *Journal of Abnormal and Social Psychology*, 1928, *23*, 118-136.

Allport, G. W., and P. E. Vernon, *Study of values: A scale for measuring the dominant interests in personality.* Boston: Houghton Mifflin Co., 1931.

APA Committee on Psychological Tests, Technical recommendations for psychological tests and diagnostic techniques, *Psychological Bulletin Supplement*, 1954, *51*, 2, Part 2, 1-38.

APA Committee on Psychological Tests, *Standards for educational and psychological tests and manuals*, Washington, D. C.: American Psychological Association, 1966.

Amrine, M. (Ed.), Special issue: Testing and public policy, *American Psychologist*, 1965, *20*, 857-1005.

Anastasi, Anne (Ed.), *Testing problems in perspective.* Washington, D. C.: American Council on Education, 1966.

Andrews, B. F., Auditory tests, *American Journal of Psychology*, 1904, *15*, 14-56.

Aschaffenburg, G., Experimentelle Studien über Associationen, *Psychologische Arbeiten*, 1896, *1*, 209-299.

Ayres, L. P., *A measuring scale for ability in spelling*, New York: Russell Sage Foundation, 1915.

Bagley, W. C., On correlation of mental and motor ability in school children, *American Journal of Psychology*, 1901, *12*, 193-205.

Bender, Lauretta, A visual motor Gestalt test and its clinical use, *Research Monograph of the American Orthopsychiatric Association*, 1938, No. 3.

Bennett, G. K., *Mechanical Comprehension Test*, New York: The Psychological Corporation, 1940.

Benton, A. L., A visual retention test for clinical use, *Archives of Neurology and Psychiatry*, 1945, *54*, 212-216.

Bernreuter, R. G., *The personality inventory*, Stanford, Calif.: Stanford University Press, 1931.

Binet, A., La perception des longeurs et des nombres chez les enfants, *Revue Philosophique*, 1890a, *30*, 68-81.

Binet, A., Perceptions d'enfants, *Revue Philosophique*, 1890b, *30*, 582-611.

Binet, A., Attention et adaptation, *L'Année Psychologique*, 1900, *6*, 248-404.

Binet, A., *L'Étude expérimentale de l'intelligence*, Paris: Schleicher, 1903.

Binet, A., Sommaire des travaux en cours à la Société de Psychologie de l'Enfant, *L'Année Psychologique*, 1904, *10*, 116-130.

Binet, A., Le développement de l'intelligence chez les enfants, *L'Année Psychologique*, 1908, *14*, 1-94.

Binet, A., Analyses bibliographique, *L'Année Psychologique*, 1911a, *17*, 477.

Binet, A., Nouvelles recherches sur la mesure du niveau intellectuel chez les enfants d'école, *L'Année Psychologique*, 1911b, *17*, 145-201.

Binet, A., and V. Henri, La mémoire des mots, *L'Année Psychologique*, 1895a, *1*, 1-23.

Binet, A., and V. Henri, La mémoire des phrases, *L'Année Psychologique*, 1895b, *1*, 24-59.

Binet, A., and V. Henri, La psychologie individuelle, *L'Année Psychologique*, 1896, *2*, 411-465.

Binet, A., and T. Simon, Sur la nécessité d'établir un diagnostic scientifique des états inférieur de l'intelligence, *L'Année Psychologique*, 1905a, *11*, 163-190.

Binet, A., and T. Simon, Méthodes nouvelles pour le diagnostic du niveau intellectual des anormaux, *L'Année Psychologique*, 1905b, *11*, 191-244.

Binet, A., and T. Simon, Application des méthodes nouvelles au diagnostic du niveau intellectuel chez des enfants normaux et anormaux d'hospice et d'école primaire, *L'Année Psychologique*, 1905c, *11*, 245-336.

Binet, A., and T. Simon, Le développement de l'intelligence chez les enfants, *L'Année Psychologique*, 1908, *14*, 1-94.

Binet, A., and N. Vaschide, Correlation des épreuves physique, *L'Année Psychologique*, 1897, *4*, 142-172.

Binet, A., and N. Vaschide, Mémoires originaux, I-XVIII, *L'Année Psychologique*, 1898, 1-315.

Bingham, W. V., Development and standardization of the Army Trade Tests, in William T. Bawden, *The Army Trade Tests*, Industrial Education Circular No. 4, Washington, D. C.: Department of the Interior, Bureau of Education, April, 1919.

Blin, Dr., Les débilités mentales, *Revue de Psychiatrie*, N.S., 1902, *5*, 337-356.

Bonser, F. G., The reasoning ability of children of the fourth, fifth and sixth school grades, *Teachers College, Columbia University, Contributions to Education*, 1910, No. 37.

Bourdon, B., Influence de l'age sur la mémoire immédiate, *Revue Philosophique*, 1894, *38*, 148-167.

Brown, W., Some experimental results in the correlation of mental abilities, *British Journal of Psychology*, 1910, *3*, 296-322.

Buck, J. N., The H-T-P test, *Journal of Clinical Psychology*, 1948, *4*, 151-159.

Buckingham, B. R., Spelling ability: Its measurement and distribution, *Teachers College, Columbia University, Contributions to Education,* No. 59, 1915.

Buros, O. (Ed.), *The Nineteen Thirty-Eight Mental Measurements Yearbook of the School of Education, Rutgers University,* New Brunswick, N. J.: Rutgers University Press, 1938.

Buros, O. (Ed.), *The Nineteen Forty Mental Measurements Yearbook,* Highland Park, N. J.: Gryphon Press, 1941.

Buros, O. (Ed.), *The Third Mental Measurements Yearbook,* Highland Park, N. J.: Gryphon Press, 1949.

Buros, O. (Ed.), *The Fourth Mental Measurements Yearbook,* Highland Park, N. J.: Gryphon Press, 1953.

Buros, O. (Ed.), *The Fifth Mental Measurements Yearbook,* Highland Park, N. J.: Gryphon Press, 1959.

Buros, O. (Ed.), *The Sixth Mental Measurements Yearbook,* Highland Park, N. J.: Gryphon Press, 1965.

Burt, C., Experimental tests of higher mental processes and their relation to general intelligence, *Journal of Experimental Pedagogy,* 1911, *1,* 93-112.

Burt, C., *Mental and scholastic tests,* London: P. S. King and Son, 1921.

Cameron, N., Reasoning, regression and communication in schizophrenics, *Psychological Monographs,* 1938, *50,* 221.

Campbell, D. T., and D. W. Fiske, Convergent and discriminant validation by the multitrait-multimethod matrix, *Psychological Bulletin,* 1959, *56,* 81-105.

Carter, L. F. (Ed.), *Psychological research on navigator training,* Report 10, Army Air Forces Aviation Psychology Program Research Reports, Washington, D. C.: U. S. Government Printing Office, 1947.

Cattell, J. McK., Mental association investigated by experiment, *Mind,* 1889, *14,* 230-250.

Cattell, J. McK., Mental tests and measurements, *Mind,* 1890, *15,* 373-381.

Cattell, J. McK., and L. Farrand, Physical and mental measurements of the students of Columbia University, *Psychological Review,* 1896, *3,* 618-648.

Cattell, R. B., The description of personality: Principles and findings in a factor analysis, *American Journal of Psychology,* 1945, *58,* 69-90.

Chadwick, E. B., Statistics of educational results, *The Museum,* 1864, *3,* 479-484.

Chauncey, H., and J. E. Dobbin, *Testing: Its place in education today,* New York: Harper and Row, 1963.

Cody, S., *Commercial tests and how to use them,* Yonkers: World Book, 1919.

Courtis, S. A., Measurement of growth and efficiency in arithmetic, *Elementary School Teacher,* 1909, *10,* 58-74, 177-199.

Courtis, S. A., *Why children succeed*, Detroit: Courtis Standard Tests, 1925.

Cowdery, K. M., Measurement of professional attitudes: Differences between lawyers, physicians, and engineers, *Journal of Personnel Research*, 1926–27, 5, 131-141.

Cron, L., and E. Kraepelin, Ueber die Messung der Auffassungsfähigkeit, *Psychologische Arbeiten*, 1899, 2, 203-325.

Cronbach, L. J., Response sets and test validity, *Educational and Psychological Measurement*, 1946, 6, 475-494.

Cronbach, L. J., Assessment of individual differences, *Annual Review of Psychology*, Vol. 7, 1956 (P. R. Farnsworth, and Quinn McNemar, Eds.), Stanford, Calif.: Annual Reviews, Inc., 1956.

Cronbach, L. J., and Goldine C. Gleser, *Psychological tests and personnel decisions*, Urbana: University of Illinois Press, 1957.

Decroly, O., and J. Degand, Les tests de Binet et Simon pour la mesure de l'intelligence: Contribution critique, *Archives de Psychologie*, 1906, 6, 27-130.

Dodge, R., in C. Murchison (Ed.), *History of psychology in autobiography*, Vol. 1, New York: Russell and Russell, 1961, pp. 116-121.

Downey, M. T., *Ben D. Wood, educational reformer*, Princeton, N. J.: Educational Testing Service, 1965.

DuBois, P. H., A test-dominated society: China, 1115 B.C.—1905 A.D., *Proceedings of the 1964 invitational conference on testing problems*, Princeton, N. J.: Educational Testing Service, 1965, pp. 3-11.

Dvorak, B. J., The new U.S.E.S. general aptitude test battery, *Journal of Applied Psychology*, 1947, 31, 372-376.

Eaton, D. B., *Civil service in Great Britain*, New York: Harper, 1880.

Ebbinghaus, H., Ueber eine neue Methode zur Prüfung geistige Fähigkeiten und ihre Anwendung bei Schulkindern., *Z. für Psychol. u Physiol. der Sinnesorgane*, 1896, 13, 401-457.

Filer, H. A., and L. J. O'Rourke, Progress in Civil Service Tests, *Journal of Personnel Research*, 1922–23, 1, 484-520.

Flanagan, J. C. (Ed.), *The aviation psychology program in the Army Air Forces*, Report 1, Army Air Forces Aviation Psychology Program Research Reports, Washington, D. C.: U. S. Government Printing Office, 1948.

Flanagan, J. C., The use of comprehensive rationales in test development, *Educational and Psychological Measurement*, 1951, 11, 151-155.

Flanagan, J. C., et al., *Design for a study of American youth*, Boston: Houghton Mifflin, 1962.

Frederiksen, N., D. R. Saunders, and Barbara Wand, The in-basket test, *Psychological Monographs*, 1957, 71, 9.

Freyd, M., The measurement of interests in vocational selection, *Journal of Personnel Research*, 1922–23, 1, 319-328.

Fullerton, G. S., and J. McK. Cattell, *On the perception of small differences with special reference to the extent, force, and time of movement,*

Philadelphia: Philosophical Series of the Publications of the University of Pennsylvania, 1892, No. 2.

Galton, F., Psychometric facts, *Nineteenth Century*, 1879, 5, 425-433.

Galton, F., *Inquiries into human faculty and its development*, New York: Macmillan, 1883.

Gelb, A., and K. Goldstein, *Psychologische Analysen Hirnpathologischer Falle*, Leipzig: Barth, 1920.

Gibson, J. J. (Ed.), Motion picture testing and research, *Army Air Forces Aviation Psychology Program Research Reports*, Report 7, Washington, D. C.: Government Printing Office, 1947.

Gilbert, J. A., Researches on the mental and physical development of school children, *Studies of the Yale Psychological Laboratory*, 1894, 2, 40-100.

Goddard, H. H., The Binet and Simon tests of intellectual capacity, *The Training School*, 1908, 5, 3-9.

Goddard, H. H., A measuring scale of intelligence, *The Training School*, 1910, 6, 146-155.

Goldsmith, Dorothy, The use of personal history blanks as a salesmanship test, *Journal of Applied Psychology*, 1922, 6, 149-155.

Goldstein, K., and M. Scheerer, Abstract and concrete behavior: An experimental study with special tests, *Psychological Monographs*, 1941, 53, No. 239.

Goodenough, F. L., *Measurement of intelligence by drawings*, Yonkers: World Book, 1926.

Graham, Frances, and Barbara Kendall, Performance of brain-damaged cases on a memory-for-designs test, *Journal of Abnormal and Social Psychology*, 1946, 41, 303-314.

Gross, A., Untersuchungen über die Schrift Gesunder und Geisteskranker, *Psychologische Arbeiten*, 1899, 2, 450-567.

Guilford, J. P., *Psychometric methods*, New York: McGraw-Hill, 1936.

Guilford, J. P., and Ruth Guilford, Personality factors S, E, M and their measurement, *Journal of Psychology*, 1936, 2, 109-127.

Gulliksen, H., *Theory of mental tests*, New York: John Wiley, 1950.

Hathaway, S. R., and J. C. McKinley, A multiphasic personality schedule (Minnesota): I. Construction of the schedule, *Journal of Psychology*, 1940, 10, 249-254.

Hathaway, S. R., and P. Meehl, *An atlas for the clinical use of the MMPI*, Minneapolis: University of Minnesota Press, 1951.

Healy, W., A pictorial completion test, *Psychological Review*, 1919, 21, 189-203.

Healy, W., and G. M. Fernald, Tests for practical mental classification, *Psychological Monographs*, 1911, 13, No. 54.

Henmon, V. A. C., Air service tests of aptitude for flying, *Journal of Applied Psychology*, 1919, 3, 103-109.

Hildreth, Gertrude H., *A bibliography of mental tests and rating scales*, New York: The Psychological Corporation, 1933.

Hillegas, M. R., A scale for the measurement of quality of English composition by young people, *Teachers College Record*, 1912, *13*, 331-384.

Hollingworth, H. L., Specialized vocational tests and methods, *School and Society*, 1915, *1*, 918-922.

Jacobs, J., Experiments on "Prehension," *Mind*, 1887, *12*, 75-79.

Jenckes, T. A., *Civil Service of the United States*. Report No. 47, 40th Congress, 2nd Session, May 25, 1868.

Jung, C. G., The association method, *American Journal of Psychology*, 1910, *21*, 219-269.

Jung, C. G., and Fr. Riklin, Untersuchungen über Assoziationen Gesunder, *Journal für Psychologie und Neurologie*, 1904, *3*, 55-83.

Kelley, T. L., Educational guidance: An experimental study in the analysis and predicting of ability of high school pupils, *Teachers College, Columbia University Contributions to Education*, 1914, No. 71.

Kelley, T. L., *Statistical Method*, New York: Macmillan, 1923.

Kent, G. H., and A. Rosanoff, The study of association in insanity, *American Journal of Insanity*, 1910, *67*, 37-96.

Knox, H. A., A scale, based on the work at Ellis Island, for estimating mental defect, *Journal of the American Medical Association*, 1914, *62*, 741-747.

Koerth, Wilhelmine, A pursuit apparatus: Eye-hand coordination, *Psychological Monographs*, 1922, *31*, 288-292.

Kohs, S. C., The block-design tests, *Journal of Experimental Psychology*, 1920, *3*, 357-376.

Kohs, S. C., *Intelligence measurement*, New York: Macmillan, 1923.

Kraepelin, E., Der psychologische Versuch in der Psychiatrie, *Psychologische Arbeiten*, 1894, *1*, 1-91.

Krueger, F., and C. Spearman, Die Korrelation zwischen verschiedenen geistigen Leistungsfähigkeiten, *Zeitschrift für Psychologie*, 1907, *44*, 50-114.

Kuder, G. F., *Kuder preference record*. Chicago: Science Research Associates, 1934.

Kuder, G. F., and M. W. Richardson, The theory of estimation of test reliability, *Psychometrika*, 1937, *2*, 151-166.

Kuhlmann, F., Experimental studies in mental deficiency, *American Journal of Psychology*, 1904, *15*, 391-446.

Laird, D. A., Detecting abnormal behavior, *Journal of Abnormal and Social Psychology*, 1925, *20*, 128-141.

Lee, J. M., *A guide to measurement in secondary schools*, New York: Appleton-Century, 1936.

Lembke, W., Über Zeichnungen von "frechen" und "schüchternen" Schulkindern, *Zeitschrift für Pädagogische Psychologie*, 1930, *31*, 459-469.

Likert, R., and W. H. Quasha, A multiple-choice revision of the Minnesota Paper Form Board, *Psychological Bulletin*, 1934, *31*, 674.

Link, H. C., *Employment Psychology*, New York: Macmillan, 1919.

Loevinger, Jane, A systematic approach to the construction and evaluation of tests of ability, *Psychological Monographs*, 1947, *61*, No. 4.

Lord, F. M., and M. R. Novick, *Statistical theories of mental test scores*, Reading, Mass.: Addison-Wesley, 1968.

Machover, Karen, *Personality projection in the drawing of the human figure*, Springfield, Ill.: Charles C. Thomas, 1949.

MacQuarrie, T. W., A mechanical ability test, *Journal of Personnel Research*, 1927, *5*, 329-337.

Martin, W. A. P., Competitive examinations in China, *North American Review*, 1870, *111*, 62-77.

Mashburn, N. C., Mashburn automatic serial action apparatus for detecting flying aptitude, *Journal of Aviation Medicine*, 1934, *5*, 155-160.

McCall, W. A., *How to measure in education*, New York: Macmillan, 1922.

McFarland, R. A., and R. C. Channell, *A revised two-hand coordination test*, Washington: CAA Airman Development Division, Report No. 36, October, 1944.

McGucken, W. J., *The Jesuits and education*, Milwaukee: Bruce Publishing Co., 1932.

McReynolds, P., *Advances in psychological assessment*, Vol. I. Palo Alto, Calif.: Science and Behavior Books, 1969.

Miner, J. B., An aid to the analysis of vocational interests, *Journal of Educational Research*, 1922, *5*, 311-323.

Moore, B. V., Personal selection of graduate engineers, *Psychological Monographs*, 1921, *30*, No. 138.

Morgan, C. D., and H. A. Murray, A method for investigating fantasies: The thematic apperception test, *Archives of Neurology and Psychiatry*, 1935, *34*, 289-306.

Moss, F. A., T. Hunt, K. T. Omwake, and M. M. Ronning, *Social intelligence test*, Washington: Center for Psychological Service, 1927.

Münsterberg, H., *Psychology and industrial efficiency*, Boston: Houghton Mifflin, 1913.

Murray, H. A., *Explorations in personality*, New York: Oxford University Press, 1938.

Murray, H. A., D. W. MacKinnon, J. G. Miller, D. W. Fiske, and Eugenia Hanfmann, *Assessment of men*, New York: Henry Holt, 1948.

O'Connor, J., *Born that way*, Baltimore: Williams and Wilkins, 1928.

Oehrn, A., Experimentelle Studien zur Individualpsychologie, *Psychologische Arbeiten*, 1896, *1*, 92-151.

OSS Assessment Staff, *Assessment of men*. Selection of personnel for the Office of Strategic Services, New York: Rinehart, 1948.

Otis, A. S., An absolute point scale for the group measure of intelligence, *Journal of Educational Psychology*, 1918, *9*, 238-61, 333-48.

Pascal, G. R., and Barbara J. Suttell, *The Bender-Gestalt test*, New York: Grune and Stratton, 1951.

Paterson, D. G., R. M. Elliott, L. D. Anderson, H. A. Toops, and D. Heidbreder, *Minnesota mechanical ability tests*, Minneapolis: The University of Minnesota Press, 1930.

Payne, A. F., *Sentence completions*, New York: New York Guidance Clinic, 1928.

Pintner, R., The mentality of the dependent child, *Journal of Educational Psychology*, 1917, 8, 220-238.

Pintner, R., and D. G. Paterson, *A scale of performance tests*, New York: Appleton, 1917.

Porteus, S. D., Mental tests for the feebleminded: A new series, *Journal of Psycho-Asthenics*, 1915, 19, 200-213.

Porteus, S. D., *The maze test and clinical psychology*, Palo Alto: Pacific Books, 1959.

Pressey, S. L., and L. W. Pressey, "Cross-out" tests with suggestions as to a group scale of the emotions, *Journal of Applied Psychology*, 1919, 3, 138-150.

Pyle, W. H., *The examination of school children*, New York: Macmillan, 1913.

Ream, M. J., *Ability to sell*, Baltimore: Williams and Wilkins, 1924.

Reis, J., Ueber einfache psychologische Versuche an Gesunden und Geisteskranken, *Psychologische Arbeiten*, 1899, 2, 587-694.

Rice, J. M., The futility of the spelling grind, *The Forum*, 1897, 23, 163-172, 409-419.

Rice, J. M., Educational research: A test in arithmetic, *The Forum*, 1902, 34, 281-297.

Rice, J. M., Educational research: The results of a test in language, *The Forum*, 1903, 35, 269-293.

Richardson, M. W., and J. M. Stalnaker, A note on the use of biserial r in test research, *Journal of General Psychology*, 1933, 8, 463-465.

Rogers, Agnes L., Experimental tests of mathematical ability and their prognostic value, *Teachers College, Columbia University, Contributions to Education*, 1918, No. 89.

Rohde, Amanda R., *The sentence completion method: Its diagnostic and clinical application to mental disorders*, New York: Ronald, 1957.

Rorschach, H., *Psychodiagnostik*, Berne: Birchen, 1921.

Rosenzweig, S., The picture-association method and its application in a study of reactions to frustration, *Journal of Personality*, 1945, 14, 3-23.

Rotter, J. B., The incomplete sentences test as a method in studying personality, *American Psychologist*, 1946, 1, 286 (Abstract).

Rotter, J. B., and Janet E. Rafferty, *Manual: The Rotter incomplete sentences blank*, New York: The Psychological Corporation, 1950.

Ruggles, A. M., A diagnostic test of aptitude for clerical office work, *Teachers College, Columbia University, Contributions to Education*, 1924, No. 148.

Rupp, H., Untersuchung zur Lehrlingsprüfung bei Siemens-Schuchert, *Berlin Psychol. Z.*, 1925, 1, 54-75.

Russell, W., and G. V. Cope, Method of rating the history of achievements of applicants, *Public Personnel Studies,* 1925, *3,* 202-219.

Sargent, Helen, Projective methods: Their origins, theory, and application in personality research, *Psychological Bulletin,* 1945, *42,* 257-293.

Schneck, M. R., The measurement of verbal and numerical abilities, *Archives of Psychology,* 1929, No. 107.

Seashore, C. E., Suggestions for tests on school children, *Educational Review,* 1901, *22,* 69-82.

Seashore, C. E., *The psychology of musical talent,* Boston: Silver, Burdett, 1919.

Seashore, R. H., Individual differences in motor skills, *Journal of General Psychology,* 1930, *3,* 38-66.

Spearman, C., The proof and measurement of association between two things, *American Journal of Psychology,* 1904a, *15,* 72-101.

Spearman, C., "General intelligence," objectively determined and measured, *American Journal of Psychology,* 1904b, *15,* 201-293.

Spearman, C., Correlation calculated from faulty data, *British Journal of Psychology,* 1910, *3,* 271-295.

Spranger, E., *Types of men* (Tr. by Paul J. W. Pigors), Halle: Max Niemeyer Verlag, 1928.

Starch, D., *Educational measurements,* New York: Macmillan, 1916.

Stenquist, J. L., Measurements of mechanical ability, *Teachers College, Columbia University, Contributions to Education,* 1923, No. 130.

Stenquist, J. L., E. L. Thorndike, and M. R. Trabue, The intellectual status of children who are public charges, *Archives of Psychology,* 1915, No. 33.

Stern, W., *Die differentielle Psychologie in ihren methodischen Grundlagen,* Leipzig: Barth, 1911.

Stern, W., *Psychologischen Methoden der Intelligenz-prüfung,* Leipzig: Barth, 1912.

Stone, C. W., Arithmetical abilities and some factors determining them, *Teachers College, Columbia University, Contributions to Education,* 1908, No. 19.

Stratton, G. M., H. C. McComas, J. E. Coover, and E. Bagby, Psychological tests for selecting aviators, *Journal of Experimental Psychology,* 1920, *3,* 405-423.

Strong, E. K., Jr., An interest test for personnel managers, *Journal of Personnel Research,* 1926, *5,* 194-203.

Strong, E. K., Jr., A vocational interest test, *The Educational Record,* 1927, *8,* 107-121.

Sylvester, R. H., The form board test, *Psychological Monographs,* 1913, *15,* No. 65.

Symonds, P. M., and C. E. Jackson, An adjustment survey, *Journal of Educational Research,* 1930, *21,* 321-330.

Taylor, Janet A., The relationship of anxiety to the conditioned eyelid response, *Journal of Experimental Psychology,* 1951, *41,* 81-92.

Terman, L. M., Genius and stupidity, *Pedagogical Seminary*, 1906, *13*, 307-373.

Terman, L. M., *The measurement of intelligence*, Boston: Houghton Mifflin, 1916.

Terman, L. M., and M. A. Merrill, *Measuring intelligence*, Boston: Houghton Mifflin, 1937.

Terman, L. M., and M. A. Merrill, *Stanford-Binet intelligence scale*, Boston: Houghton Mifflin, 1960.

Thompson, Helen B., *The mental traits of sex*, Chicago: University of Chicago Press, 1903.

Thorndike, E. L., Animal intelligence, *Psychological Review, Monograph Supplement*, 1898, 2, No. 8, 109.

Thorndike, E. L., *An introduction to the theory of mental and social measurements*, New York: Science Press, 1904.

Thorndike, E. L., Handwriting, *Teachers College Record*, 1910, *11*, No. 2.

Thorndike, E. L., The permanence of interests and their relation to abilities, *Popular Science Monthly*, 1912, *81*, 449-456.

Thorndike, E. L., The measurement of ability in reading: Preliminary scales and tests, *Teachers College Record*, 1914, *15*, 202-277.

Thorndike, E. L., *Intelligence examination for high school graduates* N.Y.: Teachers College, 1919.

Thurstone, L. L., Mental tests for prospective telegraphers, *Journal of Applied Psychology*, 1919a, 3, 110-117.

Thurstone, L. L., A standardized test for office clerks, *Journal of Applied Psychology*, 1919b, 3, 248-251.

Thurstone, L. L., A neurotic inventory, *Journal of Social Psychology*, 1930, *1*, 3-30.

Thurstone, L. L., *The reliability and validity of tests*, Ann Arbor, Mich.: Edwards, 1931a.

Thurstone, L. L., Multiple factor analysis, *Psychological Review*, 1931b, 38, 406-427.

Thurstone, L. L., *The vectors of the mind*, Chicago: University of Chicago Press, 1935.

Trabue, M. R., Completion-test language series, *Teachers College, Columbia University, Contributions to Education*, 1916, No. 77.

Vernon, P. E., and G. W. Allport, A test for personal values, *Journal of Abnormal and Social Psychology*, 1931, *26*, 231-248.

Weider, A., B. Mittelmann, D. Wechsler, and H. G. Wolff, The Cornell selectee index: A method for quick testing of selectees for the armed forces, *Journal of American Medical Association*, 1944, *124*, 224.

Weigl, E., On the psychology of the so-called process of abstraction, *Journal of Abnormal and Social Psychology*, 1941, *36*, 3-33.

Whipple, G. M., *Manual of mental and physical tests*, Baltimore: Warwick and York, 1910.

Wissler, C., The correlation of mental and physical traits, *Psychological Review, Monograph Supplement*, 1901, 3, No. 6.

Wood, B. D., *Measurement in higher education*, New York: Harcourt, Brace and World, 1923.

Woodworth, R. S., Race differences in mental traits, *Science*, N. S., 1910, *31*, 171-186.

Woodworth, R. S., Examination of emotional fitness for warfare, *Psychological Bulletin*, 1919, *16*, 59-60.

Woodworth, R. S., in C. Murchison (Ed.), *History of Psychology in Autobiography*, Vol. 2, New York: Russell and Russell, 1951, 359-381.

Woodworth, R. S., and F. L. Wells, Association tests, *Psychological Monographs*, 1911, *13*, No. 57.

Woody, C., Measurements of some achievements in arithmetic, *Teachers College, Columbia University, Contributions to Education*, 1916, No. 80.

Yerkes, R. M., Report of the Psychology Committee of the National Research Council, *Psychological Review*, 1919, *26*, 83-149.

Yerkes, R. M. (Ed.), Psychological examining in the United States Army, *Memoirs of the National Academy of Sciences*, 1921, *15*.

Yerkes, R. M., J. W. Bridges, and R. S. Hardwick, *A point scale for measuring ability*, Baltimore, Maryland: Warwick and York, 1915.

Yerkes, R. M., and J. C. Foster, *A point scale for measuring mental ability*, 1923 revision, Baltimore, Maryland: Warwick and York, 1923.

Yoakum, C. S., Basic experiments in vocational guidance, *Journal of Personnel Research*, 1921, *1*, 18-34.

CHRONOLOGY
OF PSYCHOMETRICS

1115 B. C.	Chinese testing for government positions.
1219 A. D.	Law examinations at the University of Bologna.
1599	Rules for conduct of written examinations published by Jesuit order.
1833	Competitive examinations in England for Indian civil service.
1870	Competitive examinations in U. S. Department of Interior and Treasury Department.
1879	Galton's study of association.
1883	U. S. Civil Service Commission established; Galton's *Inquiries into Human Faculty and its Development.* (introduction of term "psychometrics").
1884	Galton's Anthropometric Laboratory opened in London.
1888	Cattell's battery of tests at the University of Pennsylvania.
1891	Cattell founds Psychological Laboratory at Columbia University.
1893	Jastrow administers test battery at Columbian Exposition, Chicago.
1894	Kraepelin proposes use of tests in psychopathology.
1896	Ebbinghaus completion test; Witmer founder of first psychological clinic.
1897	Rice measures spelling achievement.
1900	College Entrance Examination Board established.
1902	Blin publishes scale for the diagnosis of mental retardation; Rice reports on arithmetic testing.
1903	Language testing by Rice.
1904	Spearman introduces correction for attenuation and two factor theory of intelligence; Woodworth studies race differences at the World's Fair, St. Louis; Thorndike's *Introduction to the Theory of Mental and Social Measurements*; Jung's studies of association.
1905	First intelligence scale published by Binet and Simon; Chinese civil service tests abolished; Terman's study of genius and stupidity.
1907	Krueger and Spearman introduce the term "reliability coefficient."

143

1908   Concept of mental age introduced in second Binet scale;
            Stone publishes first standardized achievement test
            (arithmetic).
1909   Goddard translation of the Binet Scale.
1910   Kent and Rosanoff's *The Study of Association in Insanity*;
            Whipple's *Manual of Mental and Physical Tests*;
            Thorndike Handwriting Scale; Spearman-Brown proph-
            ecy formula; Burt invents the verbal analogy.
1911   Healy and Fernald's *Tests for Practical Mental Classifica-
            tion*; Goddard Revision of Binet Scale; Woodworth-
            Wells association tests; Binet publishes revision and
            extension of his scale.
1912   Hillegas scale for measurement of English composition;
            Stern proposes concept of "Intelligenzquotient."
1913   Pyle's battery of group mental tests.
1914   Thorndike Reading Test; Knox publishes nonverbal Ellis
            Island Scale for estimating mental retardation.
1915   Stenquist Test of Mechanical Ability, Porteus Maze Test;
            Ayres' Spelling Test.
1916   Terman publishes Stanford Revision of Binet-Simon Scale;
            Link uses psychological tests in arms plant.
1917   Yerkes chairman of Committee on the Psychological Exam-
            ination of Recruits; development of Examination *a*,
            predecessor of Army Alpha; Army Trade Tests; Pintner-
            Paterson Performance Scale; Stenquist Mechanical As-
            sembly Test.
1918   Army Alpha; Woodworth Personal Data Sheet; Otis Group
            Test of Intelligence; plans made for analysis of army
            testing with punched-card machines.
1919   Seashore Measures of Musical Talent.
1920   Kohs' Block Design Test.
1921   Allport Ascendance-Submission Test; Rorschach's inkblots
            published; Burt's *Mental and Scholastic Tests*.
1922   McCall's *How to Measure in Education*; Thurstone Exami-
            nation in Clerical Work; Freyd Interest Inventory.
1923   Kelley's *Statistical Method*; Pintner General Ability Tests;
            Stanford Achievement Tests.
1924   O'Rourke employed by U. S. Civil Service Commission as
            director of research.
1926   Goodenough Draw-a-Man Test.
1927   Strong Vocational Interest Blank.
1928   Payne *Sentence Completions*.

1930	Minnesota Mechanical Ability Tests.
1931	Allport-Vernon Study of Values; Thurstone's *The Reliability and Validity of Tests*.
1934	Kuder Preference Record.
1935	Murray's Thematic Apperception Test; Buros publishes first Mental Measurements Yearbook; Vineland Social Maturity Scale; founding of the Psychometric Society; development of first test-scoring machine (IBM model 805).
1936	Guilford's *Psychometric Methods*; first Invitational Conference on Testing Problems; first issue of *Psychometrika*.
1937	Stanford-Binet revised by Terman and Merrill; Kuder and Richardson publish "K-R 20" in *Psychometrika*.
1938	Bender's *A Visual Motor Gestalt Test and its Clinical Use*; Murray's *Explorations in Personality*; Raven Progressive Matrices.
1939	Army General Classification Test; Wechsler's *The Measurement of Adult Intelligence*.
1940	Minnesota Multiphasic Personality Inventory; Bennett Mechanical Comprehension Test; *Educational and Psychological Measurement* begins publication.
1941	Goldstein-Scheerer Tests of Abstract and Concrete Thinking.
1943	Program of assessment for the selection of personnel for the Office of Strategic Services; Strong's *Vocational Interests of Men and Women*.
1946	Graham-Kendall Memory for Designs Test.
1947	Gibson's *Motion Picture Testing and Research*; Differential Aptitude Tests.
1948	Flanagan's *The Aviation Psychology Program in the Army Air Forces*; Rosenzweig Picture-Frustration Study; Educational Testing Service founded.
1950	Gulliksen's *Theory of Mental Tests*.
1954	*Technical Recommendations for Psychological Tests and Diagnostic Techniques* (APA-APGA Committee).
1957	Project Talent initiated.
1968	Lord and Novick's *Statistical Theories of Mental Test Scores*.

APPENDIX

Some Tests of Historic Interest

An Early Civil Service Examination
Civil Service Board, Department of the Interior
Washington, D. C., January 14, 1873

EXAMINATION FOR EXAMINER
OF TRADE-MARKS, PATENT OFFICE

1. What is a trade-mark, and to what applicable?
2. Who may obtain one?
3. What is the geographical extent of a trade-mark?
4. What is domicile, for the purpose of the act of July 8, 1870?
5. What are the characteristics of a trade-mark?
6. Can a geographical name, word descriptive of quality, or mere personal name, be a trade-mark? Reasons pro or con in each case.
7. What are the requirements in making application for a trade-mark?
8. What is the lifetime of a trade-mark?
9. May it be renewed, and if so, on what conditions?
10. Is a trade-mark assignable? If so, what are the conditions?
11. Has the fact that an article is patented, and thus is exclusive property, any bearing upon the question of a trade-mark on the name of the said article?
12. Can any corporate body obtain a trade-mark?
13. What valuable effect has the registration of a trade-mark?
14. Two or more applications are pending for the same trade-mark. What are the proceedings?
15. What is the course of appeal in the case above stated?
16. Application is made for a trade-mark already registered. What is the proper course of action?
17. What protection for trade-marks was afforded prior to the act of July 8, 1870?
18. Did the act of 1870 change the characteristics of a lawful trade-mark?
19. Application is made for "The Iron Boot-jack" as a trade-mark. How shall it be treated?

20. A banking company asks protection for a certain device, as a trademark, which they propose to put upon their notes. What action would you take on the application?

Comment. This is one of a large number of tests devised by the Civil Service Board that was appointed by President U. S. Grant under a rider to an appropriations bill of 1871. The Board went out of existence four years later when Congress failed to appropriate funds for the continuation of its activities. Some of the procedures developed by this Board have been followed by the permanent Civil Service Commission established under the Pendleton Act of 16 January 1883. Dorman B. Eaton, the second chairman of the original organization, was one of the three Civil Service Commissioners appointed by President Chester A. Arthur in 1883.

KELLEY'S INTEREST TEST, 1914

Name——————————————   Date—————————

1. Go through the accompanying list of magazines and put an X opposite
those with which you are not familiar, that is, opposite those of which you
have never looked through at least two numbers.

1.	All Story	36.	Leslie's Weekly
2.	American Boy	37.	Life
3.	American	38.	Lippincott's
4.	Argosy	39.	Literary Digest
5.	Atlantic Monthly	40.	McClure's
6.	Black Cat	41.	Metropolitan
7.	Blue Book	42.	Modern Priscilla
8.	Bookman	43.	Moving Picture World
9.	Cassier's	44.	Munsey's
10.	Century	45.	Musician
11.	Collier's Weekly	46.	National Geographic
12.	Commoner	47.	Outing
13.	Cosmopolitan	48.	Outlook
14.	Country Life in America	49.	Photographic Times
15.	Craftsman	50.	Pictorial Review
16.	Current Literature	51.	Popular Mechanics
17.	Delineator	52.	Popular Science Monthly
18.	Electrical World	53.	Printer's Ink
19.	Etude	54.	Puck
20.	Everybody's	55.	Red Book
21.	Good Housekeeping	56.	Review of Reviews
22.	Graphic	57.	St. Nicholas
23.	Green Book	58.	Saturday Evening Post
24.	Hampton's	59.	Science
25.	Harper's Weekly	60.	Scientific American
26.	Harper's Monthly	61.	Scribner's
27.	Hearst's	62.	Smart Set
28.	Home Needlework	63.	Strand
29.	Illustrated London News	64.	System
30.	L'Illustration	65.	Technical World
31.	Illustrierte Zeitung	66.	Theatre
32.	Industrial Engineering	67.	Woman's Home Companion
33.	International Studio	68.	Wilshire's
34.	Ladies Home Journal	69.	World's Work
35.	LaFollette's	70.	Youth's Companion

149

1.   Go through the list again, marking the five that interest you most A, B, C, D and E; A for the most interesting of all, B for the next most interesting, and so on. Do not spend much time in deciding exactly upon your preferences.

2.   Briefly tell why you particularly enjoy reading the magazine that you have marked A.

3.   Name three books which you have read in the last two years that have interested you very much. 1 _____
2 _____3 _____

4.   Suppose that you have an hour's leisure time, in what outdoor amusement would you prefer to spend it?   _____

5.   Suppose that you have an hour's leisure time, in what indoor amusement would you prefer to spend it?   _____

6.   Of the two amusements named in your answers to questions 4 and 5 which do you prefer?   _____

7.   If you had the opportunity, which one of the following would you attend, supposing each of them to be first class of its kind? Mark it A.

1. Moving picture entertainment	9. Boxing contest
2. Circus	10. Band concert
3. Football game	11. Political rally
4. Baseball game	12. Light opera
5. Track meet	13. Drama
6. Musical comedy	14. Lecture, or stereopticon
7. Vaudeville performance	lecture, on a subject
8. Grand opera	that interests you.

8.   What occupation would you prefer as a life work?   _____
Which would you like next best?   _____

9.   In the following list of words mark with a 3 those you know the meaning of perfectly and could define as a dictionary does.

If you can explain in a general way the meaning of the word and would understand it when used in a sentence mark it with a 2.

If you cannot explain its meaning but are vaguely familiar with it, mark it with a 1.

If the word is entirely new to you and unknown, mark it with a 0.

In doing this, go through the list four times, the first time marking the 3's, the second time the 2's, the third time the 1's, and the last time the 0's.

1. simile	5. Acropolis
2. primary election	6. rip saw
3. Mason and Dixon's line	7. hydrogen
4. creed	8. compound interest

9. cube root
10. paradox
11. Saracens
12. I.W.W.
13. Whigs
14. theosophy
15. toga
16. block plane
17. NaCl
18. fissure
19. equation
20. guillotine
21. prose
22. syndicalism
23. H₂O
24. transubstantiation
25. gladiator
26. debit
27. gravity cell
28. strata
29. improper fraction
30. lever
31. ragtime
32. physical valuation of railroads
33. score (in music)
34. commercial fertilizer
35. Magna Charta
36. voucher
37. ohm
38. string halt
39. fourth dimension
40. piston rod
41. Pythagorean proposition
42. single tax
43. stamen
44. hemstitch
45. Spanish Armada
46. statute of limitations
47. coherer
48. vertebrate
49. parallelogram
50. omelette
51. Reichstag
52. Commerce Court
53. states' rights
54. space bar
55. giblets
56. Australian ballot
57. mollusk
58. perspective
59. fireless cooker
60. mortgagee
61. referendum
62. Formosa

10. Tell what each of the following words means as well as you can.

a. simile————————————————————————
b. cube root——————————————————————
c. improper fraction—————————————————
d. ragtime————————————————————————
e. physical valuation of railroads————————
f. commercial fertilizer————————————————
g. ohm —————————————————————————
h. Pythagorean proposition——————————————
i. single tax————————————————————————
j. hemstitch————————————————————————
k. vertebrate————————————————————————
l. parallelogram——————————————————————
m. omelette————————————————————————

Comment. The pupils were told to answer the questions on the sheets handed to them. As much time as was needed was given; most of the pupils finished the task in 40 minutes. This seems to have been the earliest formal interest test. It had several features that were incorporated in later tests: expression of interest in magazines and activities, weighted scoring of items, and differential scores for different areas of interest—in this case, mathematics, English, and history. The use of knowledge measures (Items 9 and 10) has been advocated from time to time. Kelley (1914) reported that his interest measures definitely added to the prediction of high school grades, as compared with the use of ability tests alone.

Instructions and Items from Examination a, Form A,

U. S. Army, 1917

TEST 1

This test was administered orally. Diagrams for the first three items follow:

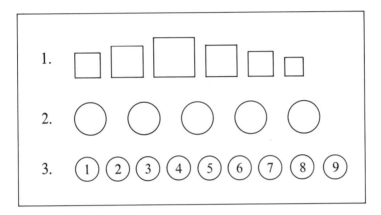

Instructions given by the examiner were:

1. "Attention! 'Attention' always means 'Pencils up!' Look at 1. When I say 'Go' (but not before), make a cross in the largest square—GO!" (Allow not over 3 seconds.)

2. "Attention! Look at 2. When I say 'Go' make a cross in the first circle and also a figure 1 in the third circle—GO!" (Allow not over 5 seconds.)

3. "Attention! Look at 3. When I say 'Go' draw a line from circle 1 to circle 4 that will pass *above* circle 2 and *below* circle 3—GO!" (Allow not over 5 seconds.)

TEST 2

Test 2, *Memory Span*, was also administered orally. Instructions to the examiner were:

Read the numbers (next page) in this test very distinctly at the rate of 1 digit per second, taking special care to avoid grouping or accenting. Allow not over 10 seconds for writing 4, 5, and 6 digit numbers. Allow not over 15 seconds for writing 7, 8, and 9 digit numbers. Proceed with the numbers of Form A (or B, etc.), giving the two 3-digit numbers, the two 4-digit numbers, the two 5-digit numbers, and so on through the two 9-digit numbers. Announce before each set the number of digits and the number of the set. Thus, begin by saying:

"Attention! Look at the directions while I read them. 'This is a test to see how many figures you can remember and write down after they are spoken. In the first row of empty squares write the first set of figures you hear, as shown in the samples; in the second row write the second set you hear, and so on.'

"In this test I shall not say 'Go,' but you are to keep your pencils raised until after I have read the whole set of figures.

"Attention!" (Hold up the hand as an example.) "Keep pencils up until I am through reading. Three figures, first set, 1 3 5." (Drop hand. Allow not over 10 seconds.)

"Attention!" (Be sure that every pencil is up.) "Three figures, second set, 6 4 1." (Drop hand. Allow not over 10 seconds.)

"Attention! Four figures, first set, 2 8 6 1."

"Attention! Four figures, second set, 5 3 9 4."

From his booklet the examinee could read instructions as given by the examiner orally:

"This is a test to see how many figures you can remember and write down after they are spoken. In the first row of empty squares write the first set of figures you hear, as shown in the samples; in the second row write the second set you hear; and so on."

Diagrams for samples, three figures and four figures are given on the next page.

```
┌─────────────────────────────────────────────────────────┐
│                                                           │
│   Sample one  . . . . . . . . . . .   ┌─┬─┬─┐             │
│                                       │4│7│5│             │
│                                       └─┴─┴─┘             │
│   Sample two  . . . . . . . . . . .   ┌─┬─┬─┐             │
│                                       │8│1│4│             │
│                                       └─┴─┴─┘             │
│  ─────────────────────────────────────────────────       │
│                  ⎧ First set     . . . . .   ┌─┬─┬─┐      │
│  Three figures:  ⎨                           └─┴─┴─┘      │
│                  ⎩ Second set  . . . . .     ┌─┬─┬─┐      │
│                                              └─┴─┴─┘      │
│                  ⎧ First set     . . . .   ┌─┬─┬─┬─┐      │
│  Four figures:   ⎨                         └─┴─┴─┴─┘      │
│                  ⎩ Second set  . . . .     ┌─┬─┬─┬─┐      │
│                                            └─┴─┴─┴─┘      │
│                                                           │
└─────────────────────────────────────────────────────────┘
```

Directions for Tests 3 through 10 were read aloud by the examiner as the examinees looked at them. The examiner then said "Ready—GO!" and, after the time allowed was over, "STOP! Turn over the page to Test 4." (or whatever the number of the next test might be).

Directions and a few items of each of these tests follow:

TEST 3

The words

MORNING THE RISES EVERY SUN

in that order don't make a sentence; but they would make a sentence if put in the right order:

THE SUN RISES EVERY MORNING

and this statement is true.

Again, the words

ANIMAL A IS THE RARE DOG

would make a sentence if put in the order:

THE DOG IS A RARE ANIMAL

but this statement is false.

Below are twenty mixed-up sentences. Some of them are true and some are false. When I say "go," take these sentences one at a time. Decide what each sentence *would* say if the words were straightened out, but don't write them yourself. Then, if what it would say is true, draw a line under the word "true"; if what it would say is false, draw a line under the word "false." If you cannot be sure, guess. The two samples are already marked as they should be. Begin with No. 1 and work right down the page until time is called.

SAMPLES $\begin{cases} \text{morning the rises every sun} \\ \text{animal a is the rare dog} \end{cases}$ _____ true—false
        animal a is the rare dog _____ <u>true</u>—false
1. wood guns of made are_____true—false 1
2. people are many candy of fond_____true—false 2
3. war in are useful airplanes the_____true—false 3

TEST 4

Get the answers to these examples as quickly as you can.
Use the side of this page to figure on if you need· to.

SAMPLES $\begin{cases} 1 \quad \text{How many are 5 men and 10 men?} \\ 2 \quad \text{If you walk 4 miles an hour for 3} \end{cases}$ ___Answer (15)
  hours, how far do you walk?_____Answer (12)
1. How many are 30 men and 7 men?_____Answer (   )
2. If you save $7 a month for 4 months, how much will you save?_____Answer (   )
3. If 24 men are divided into squads of 8, how many squads will there be?_____Answer (   )

TEST 5

Notice the sample sentence:
    People hear with the   eyes   <u>ears</u>   nose   mouth
The correct word is ears, because it makes the truest sentence.
    In each of the sentences below, you have four choices for the last word. Only one of them is correct. In each sentence draw a line under the one of these four words which makes the truest sentence. If you cannot be sure, guess. The two samples are already marked as they should be.

SAMPLES $\begin{cases} \text{People hear with the   eyes   } \underline{\text{ears}} \text{   nose   mouth} \\ \text{France is in } \underline{\text{Europe}} \text{ Asia Africa Australia} \end{cases}$
1. The snow comes in   winter   fall   summer   spring
2. The lungs are for   seeing   breathing   digestion   hearing
3. Milk comes from   oxen   cows   trees   vines

TEST 6

If the two words of a pair mean the same or nearly the same, draw a line under same. If they mean the opposite or nearly the opposite, draw a line under opposite. If you cannot be sure, guess. The two samples are already marked as they should be.

SAMPLES { good-bad ———————————————— same—opposite
{ little-small ——————————————— same—opposite
1. empty-full ——————————————— same—opposite
2. fall-rise ————————————————— same—opposite
3. confess-admit ——————————————— same—opposite

TEST 7

This is a test of common sense. Below are ten questions. Four answers are given to each question. You are to look at the answers carefully; then make a cross before the best answer to each question, as in the sample:

SAMPLE | Why do we use stoves? Because
—they look well
—they are black
✗ they keep us warm
—they are made of iron

Here the third answer is the best one and is marked with a cross. Begin with No. 1 and keep on until time is called.

1. Why ought every man to be educated? Because
   —Roosevelt was educated
   —it makes a man more useful
   —it costs money
   —some educated people are wise

2. Why ought a grocer to own an automobile? Because
   —it looks pretty
   —it is useful in his business
   —it uses rubber tires
   —it saves railroad fare

6. Why is the telephone more useful than the telegraph?   Because
    ——it gets a quicker answer
    ——it uses more miles of wire
    ——it is a more recent invention
    ——telephone wires can be put under ground

7. Why are war-ships painted gray? Because gray paint
    ——is cheaper than any other color
    ——is more durable than other colors
    ——does not show dirt
    ——makes the ships harder to see

TEST 8

In the lines below, each number is gotten in a certain way from the numbers coming before it. Study out what this way is in each line, and then write in the space left for it the number that should come next. The first two lines are already filled in as they should be.

SAMPLES	{ 2,	4,	6,	8,	10,	12
	{ 11,	12,	14,	15,	17,	18
	5,	6,	7,	8,	9,	———
	9,	11,	13,	15,	17,	———
	12,	10,	8,	6,	4,	———

TEST 9

SAMPLES | sky—blue: grass—(grow, <u>green</u>, cut, dead)
               | fish—swims: man—(boy, woman, <u>walks</u>, girl)
               | day—night: white—(red, <u>black</u>, clear, pure)

In each of the lines below, the first two words have a certain relation. Notice that relation and draw a line under the one word in the parenthesis which has that particular relation to the third word. Begin with No. 1 and mark as many sets as you can before time is called.

1   cradle—baby: stable—(horse, man, dog, eat)————————1
2   man—home: bird—(nest, fly, insect, tree)————————2
3   ear—hear: eye—(hair, blue, see, eyebrow)————————3

TEST 10

Draw a line under the largest number and also under the smallest number in every column on the page.

Samples		Begin Here							
34	31	12	47	75	41	49	57	14	45
79	48	64	56	11	91	54	53	50	77
87	66	17	29	24	16	88	27	93	46
68	26	23	61	55	12	42	15	84	73
25	60	70	69	37	36	29	97	44	38
82	98	33	20	39	75	22	58	90	54
27	33	93	71	38	18	79	19	32	70
30	23	45	68	49	60	43	85	74	89
19	52	87	48	88	92	35	81	17	42
24	78	28	26	15	96	47	57	91	31

WOODWORTH'S PERSONAL DATA SHEET, 1918

Answer the questions by underlining "Yes" when you mean yes, and by underlining "No" when you mean no. Try to answer every question.

1.	Do you usually feel well and strong?	YES	NO
2.	Do you usually sleep well?	YES	NO
3.	Are you often frightened in the middle of the night?	YES	NO
4.	Are you troubled with dreams about your work?	YES	NO
5.	Do you have nightmares?	YES	NO
6.	Do you have too many sexual dreams?	YES	NO
7.	Do you ever walk in your sleep?	YES	NO
8.	Do you have the sensation of falling when going to sleep?	YES	NO
9.	Does your heart ever thump in your ears so that you cannot sleep?	YES	NO
10.	Do ideas run through your head so that you cannot sleep?	YES	NO
11.	Do you feel well rested in the morning?	YES	NO
12.	Do your eyes often pain you?	YES	NO
13.	Do things ever seem to swim or get misty before your eyes?	YES	NO
14.	Do you often have the feeling of suffocating?	YES	NO
15.	Do you have continual itchings in the face?	YES	NO
16.	Are you bothered much by blushing?	YES	NO
17.	Are you bothered by fluttering of the heart?	YES	NO
18.	Do you feel tired most of the time?	YES	NO
19.	Have you ever had fits of dizziness?	YES	NO
20.	Do you have queer, unpleasant feelings in any part of the body?	YES	NO
21.	Do you ever feel an awful pressure in or about the head?	YES	NO
22.	Do you often have bad pains in any part of the body? Where? _____	YES	NO
23.	Do you have a great many bad headaches?	YES	NO
24.	Is your head apt to ache on one side?	YES	NO
25.	Have you ever fainted away?	YES	NO
26.	Have you often fainted away?	YES	NO
27.	Have you ever been blind, half-blind, deaf or dumb for a time?	YES	NO

28. Have you ever had an arm or leg paralyzed?	YES	NO
29. Have you ever lost your memory for a time?	YES	NO
30. Did you have a happy childhood?	YES	NO
31. Were you happy when 14 to 18 years old?	YES	NO
32. Were you considered a bad boy?	YES	NO
33. As a child did you like to play alone better than to play with other children?	YES	NO
34. Did the other children let you play with them?	YES	NO
35. Were you shy with other boys?	YES	NO
36. Did you ever run away from home?	YES	NO
37. Did you ever have a strong desire to run away from home?	YES	NO
38. Has your family always treated you right?	YES	NO
39. Did the teachers in school generally treat you right?	YES	NO
40. Have your employers generally treated you right?	YES	NO
41. Do you know of anybody who is trying to do you harm?	YES	NO
42. Do people find fault with you more than you deserve?	YES	NO
43. Do you make friends easily?	YES	NO
44. Did you ever make love to a girl?	YES	NO
45. Do you get used to new places quickly?	YES	NO
46. Do you find your way about easily?	YES	NO
47. Does liquor make you quarrelsome?	YES	NO
48. Do you think drinking has hurt you?	YES	NO
49. Do you think tobacco has hurt you?	YES	NO
50. Do you think you have hurt yourself by going too much with women?	YES	NO
51. Have you hurt yourself by masturbation (self-abuse)?	YES	NO
52. Did you ever think you had lost your manhood?	YES	NO
53. Have you ever had any great mental shock?	YES	NO
54. Have you ever seen a vision?	YES	NO
55. Did you ever have the habit of taking any form of "dope"?	YES	NO
56. Do you have trouble in walking in the dark?	YES	NO
57. Have you ever felt as if someone was hypnotizing you and making you act against your will?	YES	NO
58. Are you ever bothered by the feeling that people are reading your thoughts?	YES	NO
59. Do you ever have a queer feeling as if you were not your old self?	YES	NO
60. Are you ever bothered by a feeling that things are not real?	YES	NO

61. Are you troubled with the idea that people are watching you on the street? YES NO
62. Are you troubled with the fear of being crushed in a crowd? YES NO
63. Does it make you uneasy to cross a bridge over a river? YES NO
64. Does it make you uneasy to go into a tunnel or subway? YES NO
65. Does it make you uneasy to have to cross a wide street or open square? YES NO
66. Does it make you uneasy to sit in a small room with the door shut? YES NO
67. Do you usually know just what you want to do next? YES NO
68. Do you worry too much about little things? YES NO
69. Do you think you worry too much when you have an unfinished job on your hands? YES NO
70. Do you think you have too much trouble in making up your mind? YES NO
71. Can you do good work while people are looking on? YES NO
72. Do you get rattled easily? YES NO
73. Can you sit still without fidgeting? YES NO
74. Does your mind wander badly so that you lose track of what you are doing? YES NO
75. Does some particular useless thought keep coming into your mind to bother you? YES NO
76. Can you do the little chores of the day without worrying over them? YES NO
77. Do you feel you must do a thing over several times before you can drop it? YES NO
78. Are you afraid of responsibility? YES NO
79. Do you feel like jumping off when you are on a high place? YES NO
80. At night are you troubled with the idea that somebody is following you? YES NO
81. Do you find it difficult to pass urine in the presence of others? YES NO
82. Do you have a great fear of fire? YES NO
83. Do you ever feel a strong desire to go and set fire to something? YES NO
84. Do you ever feel a strong desire to steal things? YES NO
85. Did you ever have the habit of biting your finger nails? YES NO
86. Did you ever have the habit of stuttering? YES NO

87. Did you ever have the habit of twitching your face, neck or shoulders?	YES	NO
88. Did you ever have the habit of wetting the bed?	YES	NO
89. Are you troubled with shyness?	YES	NO
90. Have you a good appetite?	YES	NO
91. Is it easy to make you laugh?	YES	NO
92. Is it easy to get you angry?	YES	NO
93. Is it easy to get you cross or grouchy?	YES	NO
94. Do you get tired of people quickly?	YES	NO
95. Do you get tired of amusements quickly?	YES	NO
96. Do you get tired of work quickly?	YES	NO
97. Do your interests change frequently?	YES	NO
98. Do your feelings keep changing from happy to sad and from sad to happy without any reason?	YES	NO
99. Do you feel sad or low-spirited most of time?	YES	NO
100. Did you ever have a strong desire to commit suicide?	YES	NO
101. Did you ever have heart disease?	YES	NO
102. Did you ever have St. Vitus's dance?	YES	NO
103. Did you ever have convulsions?	YES	NO
104. Did you ever have anemia badly?	YES	NO
105. Did you ever have dyspepsia?	YES	NO
106. Did you ever have asthma or hay fever?	YES	NO
107. Did you ever have a nervous breakdown?	YES	NO
108. Have you ever been afraid of going insane?	YES	NO
109. Has any of your family been insane, epileptic or feeble-minded?	YES	NO
110. Has any of your family committed suicide?	YES	NO
111. Has any of your family had a drug habit?	YES	NO
112. Has any of your family been a drunkard?	YES	NO
113. Can you stand pain quietly?	YES	NO
114. Can you stand the sight of blood?	YES	NO
115. Can you stand disgusting smells?	YES	NO
116. Do you like outdoor life?	YES	NO

INDEX OF NAMES

INDEX OF SUBJECTS

Color Sorting test, 109
Columbia College, 125
Columbia University, 22, 64, 76
Columbian Exposition, testing by
  Jastrow, 23
completion test:
  Ebbinghaus, 26-27, 37
  pictorial, 53
  Trabue, 89
Complex Coordination test, 121
computers, electronic, 119-120
construct validity, 116
construction problem (OSS), 111
content validity, 116
Cooperative Test Service, 118, 125
Cornell Selectee Index, 121
creativity, measurement of, 92
criterion-related validity, 115
criticisms of testing, 130-131

differential batteries, 123-124
  Chicago Primary Mental
    Abilities, 124
  Differential Aptitude tests, 124
  Flanagan Aptitude Classification
    test, 124
  GATB, 124
  Guilford-Zimmerman Aptitude
    Survey, 124
digit-symbol substitution test, 53
Discrimination Reaction Time
  test, 122
Division of Evaluation and
  Measurement, APA, 128
Draw-a-Man test, 56, 57, 106, 144
dynamometer pressure, 17, 90

educational achievement tests,
  Binet's plan for, 39
educational examination for
  diagnosing retardation, 34-35

Educational Testing Service,
  118, 125
Ellis Island Scale, 52-53, 144
Examination a, 63-64
Examination in Clerical Work,
  Thurstone, 144

faculty psychology, 47
feature profile, 53
Finger Dexterity test, 91
finger paintings, 108
forced choice principle, 97
form board, Seguin, 53-54
form board test, 52-53
Forum, The, Rice's publications
  in, 69
free association test, 103
Fullerton-Cattell theorem, 72

Galton professorship of
  eugenics, 14
Galton whistle, 12
GATB, 124
General Ability tests, Pintner, 144
Greece and Rome, examinations
  in, 8
Group Intelligence Scale, Otis, 68,
  118, 144

Hampshire village school,
  Spearman's testing in, 42
Handwriting Scale, Thorndike,
  71, 144
hearing, 20
homogeneity, 115
H-T-P test, 108

Illinois Fair Employment
  Commission, 130
incomplete sentence tests, 107
index of reliability, 45
Ingenuity test, 50